ALSO BY JOHN DEMERS

The Community Kitchen's Complete Guide to Gourmet Coffee

Arnaud's Creole Cookbook

BY

John DeMers

WITH A PREFACE BY *Archie Casbarian*

DRAWINGS BY RODICA PRATO

SIMON AND SCHUSTER

NEW YORK · LONDON · TORONTO · SYDNEY · TOKYO

Library of Congress Cataloging-in-Publication Data

DeMers, John, date.
  Arnaud's creole cookbook.

  Includes index.
   1. Cookery, American—Louisiana style.
2. Cookery—Louisiana—New Orleans.
3. Cookery, Creole.   4. Arnaud's (Restaurant)—
History.   I. Title.
TX715.D3818   1988   641.509763'35
87-26633
ISBN 0-671-63024-5

Acknowledgments

First and foremost, I would like to thank Archie and Jane Casbarian for building on several years of casual friendship by inviting me into their Arnaud's family. They resolutely found time for me and my queries amid the nonstop crisis control known as running a restaurant. My gratitude also goes out to executive chef Christian Gille, who wrestled his stacks of commercial recipes into workable home proportions.

For research into Count Arnaud and his family, the Historic New Orleans Collection, the Greater New Orleans Public Library, and the files of the New Orleans Times Picayune-States Item proved invaluable. And for helping give form to all this research, I thank my editor, Carole Lalli, and her assistants at Simon and Schuster, first Nancy Kalish and later Kerri Conan.

Apart from the restaurant, the libraries, and the publishing house, I must express appreciation to my wife, Sandra, and my children, Sara and Michael. They showed great understanding during the two years I spent every waking minute away from my main employ digging through the past and present of Arnaud's.

To
Ralph S. O'Connor,
PARTNER AND DEAR FRIEND
—Archie Casbarian

Contents

The Basics · 65

The Main Ingredients · 73

The Vegetables · 83

The Flavorings · 91

The Recipes · 97

The art of cooking is the soul of festivity at all times and to all ages.

—Arnaud Cazenave

Preface

Giving new life to a wonderful old restaurant has been a lot of fun and a lot of hard work for my family, my talented staff, and me. During the past eight years of painstaking restoration, research, and improvement, our cuisine has remained, as always, the soul of Arnaud's. It is a cuisine that many have loyally supported over the years and one that has elicited numerous requests for recipes.

We are most grateful to our many fans and, in response, want to share our cuisine with them. If you have never been to Arnaud's, we hope one of these recipes will entice you to visit us. If you have been to Arnaud's, these recipes will hopefully rekindle fond memories and encourage you to come back again soon.

Bon Appétit!

ARCHIE A. CASBARIAN

Introduction

$\mathcal{J}$ first met Archie Casbarian in 1980, just two years after he had leased Arnaud's in the French Quarter and embarked on the $2.5 million restoration that would turn this sadly neglected landmark back into a living, breathing, grand restaurant. Before I even shook his hand, however, I had to adjust to the dramatic change his commitment had made. Arnaud's was a world apart from the place I'd visited for the first time shortly before he appeared on the scene.

As a native New Orleanian, I had grown up with the legends of Count Arnaud and his eccentric daughter, Germaine. My parents had regularly dined at Arnaud's for evenings away from the children. As one of the children they sought to escape, I did not visit the restaurant myself until I had a very special date in college.

Having regaled my sweetheart with all the best Arnaud's anecdotes, I led her into what could only be called a disaster. The one waiter on duty deposited us in the Richelieu Bar and then forgot us for two hours, in spite of the empty tables all around. When he finally seated us, he persuasively promoted Shrimp Arnaud and Trout Meunière, the house specialties to be sure, but almost certainly the only order the lonely cook could any longer handle. After serving our amazingly nondescript meals, the waiter actually excused himself, saying he had some errands to run but would be back later that evening. All through the bizarre experience, the only other diner was a stubble-bearded derelict nursing a bowl of gumbo at a tumbledown table in the corner.

When my wife and I met Archie and Jane Casbarian that spring night in 1980, I still had much to learn about food in general and Arnaud's in particular. But the contrast to my college memory was overwhelming. Gone were the dark shadows, the inappropriate arches, the filthy panes of window glass; gone as well the antiquated cashier's cage, the overworked menu, and the underworked service staff. In their place were a jewel-box dining room, an impeccably drilled yet unobtrusive staff, fresh flowers at every turn, and the wonderful food people remembered even though it had not been wonderful for many years.

As a newsman, I sensed even then a story worth telling. Six years later, as a food editor and author, I discovered that the tale verged on the astounding. The long-departed Count Arnaud proved an incredible man who more than deserved the title he never truly claimed. Germaine emerged as dramatic and fascinating but ultimately simply sad, a character who might have resulted from a collaboration by Chekhov and Tennessee Williams, with a restaurant the setting of the tragedy. And the Casbarians, while happier and certainly not eccentric, shared the flair for theater both the Count and his daughter had revered. Most important, they had the perseverance to carry it off in a tough modern world.

I make no pretense of objectivity when it comes to Arnaud's. I love the way it was and the incredible events that happened there.

I even love the oft-told tales of events that *never* really happened, for such is the nature of legend. Most of all, I love the fact that once again any diner can pass through these doors and savor dishes, service, and atmosphere that survive almost nowhere else in the world.

—John DeMers

The Making of Magic

$\mathcal{M}$ ost businesses go through a Mom-and-Pop phase if they start small enough, and most go through a Father-and-Son phase if they last long enough. Arnaud's adds luster to the history of fine dining with the most colorful, most improbable father-daughter saga imaginable. Both Count Arnaud and his daughter Germaine exhibited a flair for culinary creation that overshadowed the fact that neither was an accomplished cook. Both showed a genius for the pure theater behind raising the curtain on a restaurant each day and making the magic happen anew. And both drew their considerable energies from one incomparable city, flinging the energies back with a degree of passion that left lesser characters foundering.

Perhaps it was their French sensibility that saved Leon Bertrand Arnaud Cazenave and Germaine Cazenave Wells from a fate shared by many on the banks of the Mississippi. Their ancestors had, after all, fashioned a life-style based on looking life in the eye without flinching, reacting with dark humor and disdain rather than fear or immobilizing despair.

Throughout their long lives, father and daughter saw global reputations shaken by shifting fortune, legal turmoil and close personal tragedy. Despite three years of lung cancer, the Count was a regular at his restaurant until six weeks before his death. Germaine made one last regal turn just three months before her own death, defying a host of physical and mental deteriorations reflected so sadly in her landmark's fall from grace.

This is their story, a story with enough blemishes to make it real but not so many as to obscure their achievement. And this is also a tribute to the remarkable and unlikely fact that after their deaths their story continues, lunch and dinner, on Bienville Street in New Orleans' fabled French Quarter.

Arnaud Cazenave was born in Bosdarros, France, on June 27, 1876—taking, it seems, from the very soil a zest for living and a fascination with perfection. Bosdarros was far more than just a village on the outskirts of the famed city of Pau, residence of the kings of Navarre. It was a hamlet whose charming church and quaint houses were flanked by the grandeur of the Pyrenees and cradled by the lovely vineyards of southwest France.

Arnaud attended preparatory school at Salice de Béarn and completed his studies at the Lycée Napoléon in Paris, speaking all the while of pursuing a career in medicine. Yet even though he possessed two of the traits most often associated with that profession—a better-than-average mind and a richer-than-average store of compassion—something about the plan deeply disturbed him. The doctor still played a respected role in nearly every French village near the close of the nineteenth century, yet neither his grueling work schedule nor his limited earning potential appealed well enough to a young man already dreaming of a nobility to which he had not been born. He cast about for a more fitting future.

Paris, with its generations of family-run businesses and its hush-hush social structures, seemed a closed book to Arnaud. So, at twenty-four he set out for the United States at the invitation of relatives. He still talked of becoming a doctor but he latched onto a job selling champagne the moment his funds got low enough to justify abandoning his intention.

Arnaud found his stride almost as soon as he set foot in turn-of-the-century New York. The sheer crazy promise of it all appealed to his growing entrepreneurial spirit. He regularly traveled out from the city, hawking his high-priced wares, poking at the limitations of this exciting new world. Those limitations seemed to crumble when a selling trip took him to New Orleans. The year was 1902.

The Gallic flavor of this already historic Creole city appealed to Arnaud; New Orleans struck him as having the romance of Paris but not its endless economic roadblocks. The city had learned its earliest lessons under the French, who gave world-class courses in gaudy social functions, governmental corruption, and a degree of tolerance that led to few restrictions on behavior. This education continued under Spanish rule, which added some lovely wrought iron to the city's architecture and an influx of even more vagabonds from the far-flung corners of the earth to its population. Yet for all the swirling celebration under two colonial rulers, the worldly-wise city saved its golden age of sinfulness for its absorption by the Americans.

Arnaud found New Orleans intoxicating, particularly the French Quarter, to which he naturally gravitated. The city was full of gambling houses, smoky havens for down-and-out survivors of riverboat gaming days. Most betting parlors were officially called bars, though their real activities often spilled into the street. And most bars were called coffeehouses, though not a cup of the locally favored dark French brew was ever consumed inside. Cocktails were invented in New Orleans and served alongside a host of other pungent potables: cobblers, juleps, cold punches, and lemonade during the hot, humid summers; hot toddies and flaming neguses during the cold, wet winters.

Quarrels, fistfights, and flashing knives were common, with more serious disputes finding final resolution under the "dueling oaks" at City Park. Drinkers with cooler heads could settle back to the new sound of jazz being played on a street that took its name from the New Basin Canal or seek out the pricy female companion-ship of Storyville. The nation's only legal red-light district was at its height when Arnaud Cazenave hit town, its gaslit rooms decked out in red plush and its Blue Book describing each girl with roguish double entendre. Storyville was the place to see—but not be seen in—in New Orleans for most of Arnaud's early life here.

What intrigued the young man most, however, was the enthu-siasm the city reserved for mealtime. With the possible exception of drinking, nothing seemed to hold quite the allure of putting away large portions of pompano, crawfish, crab, and local game birds, all made dazzling by Creole spices and presented with fruits and veg-etables that arrived by ship from all around the world.

Arnaud felt completely at home with the meticulous care of this food's preparation; it was, after all, a French legacy. But he was excited too by the influence of Spain and Spanish America on the local cuisine, including rice and tomato dishes, saffron, cumin, and hot peppers, and the whole new perspective brought from Africa by the now-freed slaves. Yams, peanuts, and okra were part of this exotic heritage, with the latter giving its African name to one of the city's most famous nourishments—gumbo.

Under the influence of such rare bounty, Arnaud quickly set-tled on a dream to own a restaurant and serve dishes fit "for the best of men." But if the dream came easily, the reality most as-suredly did not. There was always the matter of capital, no small affair to a young man working in a strange town at his first real job. And there was plenty of potential competition, starting with already well-known Antoine's and winding through dozens of eateries, rich and poor. Founded in 1840, Antoine's was already in its second generation of proprietors, with its widest fame still waiting for the third. At the other extreme, oysters, "poor boy" sandwiches, pickled eggs, cold shrimp in spicy sauces, and steaming cups of gumbo were passed through tumbledown windows to laborers who downed them at the side of the muddy street.

Arnaud's ambitions for his own eatery were extravagant, and it took lean living and hard work to raise his capital. Branching out from champagne and liquor sales (and broadening his knowledge as well), Arnaud found work in old Creole restaurants like La Loui-siane and in old Creole hotels like the Bush and the Grunewald.

When the money and conditions were finally right, nearly a decade later, he took his first big leap into the business he had chosen— leasing the Old Absinthe House on Bourbon Street. The café he opened on this time-honored site was an immediate money machine.

Though drinking had long been the highlight of any night at the Absinthe House, patrons soon reveled in Arnaud's French food. They especially responded to one of his innovations, the serving of a small bottle of red wine with every meal. And they blossomed under the warmth of his old-world charm. Arnaud's reputation as a bon vivant, an unequaled raconteur, and a connoisseur of food, drink, clothing, and entertainment earned him a nickname that stayed with him for the rest of his life. "Count Arnaud" his friends and customers called him, or sometimes simply "the Count." Few newcomers to New Orleans ever realized there was no château or noble lineage waiting back home in Bosdarros, France.

The cash pouring in from the Absinthe House allowed Arnaud to buy the two things he wanted most. The first was a home fit for a Count, on a wide, tree-shaded avenue known as Esplanade. The twenty-two-room mansion featured a Turkish bath and a swimming pool on the roof, not to mention a cavernous cellar packed with hand-picked wines. Arnaud even added a tower later so his wife— known in the community as "Lady Irma"—could get a clear view of Mardi Gras parades.

The Count's second purchase was the one destined to seal his fame and fortune. Through his wide circle of friends and even wider circle of patrons, Arnaud heard of an old warehouse on Bienville Street that was coming onto the market. His friends passed him the news because they knew of his interest in opening a restaurant, but they quickly pointed out that the building at 813 Bienville was surrounded by the "wrong kinds of neighbors." After more than fifteen years in the French Quarter, Arnaud knew all too well that this warning could apply to almost any address. And he insisted to the worst doomsayers that decent people would venture "almost anywhere" for good food.

From the beginning, in 1918, it was obvious that Arnaud's was a unique restaurant—even in a city increasingly noted for its diversity. The Count's first chef was a woman known as Madame Pierre, who established a basic menu philosophy that married the finer points of French and Spanish cuisine. Arnaud himself took on the task of educating his patrons, preaching that great food should be a pleasure and "not a task to get over with in a hurry." Despite his genteel demeanor, he could be heard reprimanding businessmen who whipped through their meals in order to return to the pursuit of profit. "How can you tell this food is delicious," the Count asked one who had showered him with compliments, "if you fail to even taste it?"

Great chefs came and went at Arnaud's, yet the cuisine remained consistently incomparable. The reason was that Count Arnaud, once established as a proprietor as well as a symbol of the good life, had an instinct for ingredient combinations that would become legendary. He rarely ventured into his restaurant's kitchen, yet he knew in an instant whether a recipe would work. Spinning off from traditional shrimp rémoulade, for instance, the Count invented Shrimp Arnaud in his office and sent the formula, scribbled on a piece of paper, down to his chef. When someone asked why he didn't prepare the dish himself, Arnaud replied simply, "I'm not a cook. I give the outline."

And so it went. The man who insisted he was not a cook developed a tableful of New Orleans' most renowned dishes—Filet de Truite Vendôme, Suprême de Volaille en Papillote, Oysters Bienville, and Filet Mignon Clemenceau. Small wonder the city's financial leaders and colorful public officials came to view Arnaud's as the place to celebrate christenings, debutante parties, weddings, and business deals, along with more than a few divorces and wine-soaked wakes. And small wonder these locals soon were joined by entertainers and sports personalities visiting the city from around the world.

For many of these Arnaud's revelers, the mandatory finale to every feast was Café Brûlot, and it remains so to this day. In the 1920s and 1930s the devilish flaming coffee drink was served with incredible flair by an Arnaud's headwaiter named Cézar. A veteran of the French Foreign Legion who had labored in no small number of horrid locales, Cézar came up with a little tune reminiscent of Offenbach's *La Belle Hélène* and tacked on a hodgepodge of words that didn't quite translate in any known language. This serenade, with a host of histrionic gestures, made Cézar's ladling of the flaming Brûlot a ceremony few could forget:

En revenant du sans vree mon
Jubilant! Jubilant!
Pain pain pi na go
La cabinetre
En revenant du sans vree mon
On on on on on!

Like many another public personality, the Count fashioned an image he felt would serve his product, refined that image with the aid of reaction, and eventually exaggerated it beyond any original intent. Nevertheless it was based solidly on the way he thought, the way he acted, the way he chose to live.

Arnaud loved to sleep late, explaining to friends that mornings "bothered" him and that he truly preferred the darkness. Only at night, he would say, were people free from the cares of the day and able to be at their best. It was then that he loved to move among them.

When he did awake in his palace on Esplanade, Arnaud immediately fortified himself with a pint of vintage champagne. This was the only way to start the day right, he insisted, even though after age sixty-five he switched to orange juice on his doctor's orders. "At first it didn't taste right," he observed to anyone who inquired of the change. "But orange juice is not too bad once you get used to it."

The Count tried his best to limit business to the restaurant, steering the trainloads of purveyors and promoters to that address alone. But there remained a few details that had to be taken care of away from Arnaud's glittering chandeliers. These the Count dealt with in his own original style. Haircuts, for example, were an essential part of a cultured man's appearance, so the Count installed a barber chair in his mansion and summoned his man with the shears whenever needed.

Late in the afternoon, or early in the evening, Arnaud would appear at the restaurant, almost always wearing a white carnation in his lapel and carrying an expensive Havana cigar, which he used mostly as a prop in conversation. He would wander from table to table, having the waiters set up French 75s or Ambrosias (which were gin or apple brandy topped with champagne—his own concoctions) for his favored guests while satisfying himself with a fifty-fifty mix of bourbon and thick black coffee. The Count was known to drink up to twenty-eight of these a night, and he told friends it was his prescription for a long and healthy life. Meeker souls, he conceded, should switch after five or six cups to the tamer pleasures of scotch and soda.

Never a meek soul himself, even when illness or turmoil laid him low, Arnaud seemed to fight against the close of each long night. When business was finished, sometime after midnight, he was known to round up a raucous army of admirers—including several of his waiters and bartenders—and lead an assault on Bourbon Street's saloons. Delivery boys and early workers at the restaurant were as likely as not to spot the Count on the street, still searching for his car in the blinding morning light.

In keeping with his popularity at tableside, Arnaud was quite a philosopher and a shrewd observer of Louisiana's favorite sport— politics at any and every level. He was progressive in his thinking and motivational in his approach, constantly urging young men with any sort of talent or style to start businesses of their own.

Sometimes he backed his encouragements with cash, other times with a savvy touch of psychology. While he contributed to scores of civic causes, Arnaud was most famous for his handouts to down-and-out bums who turned up at the doors of his restaurant. Once, after handing a hungry man a hundred dollars, the Count heard a friend disparage his "misplaced generosity." Angered by this, he wagered an additional hundred he would hear from the recipient himself that his generosity was not misplaced. Within six months, the derelict had found a job and repaid the Count every penny. So did the doubting wealthy acquaintance.

When money was not the primary issue, Arnaud had a talent for finding what was. One of his friends, for example, was a New Orleans liquor salesman who dreamed of owning a restaurant. Yet with a large family to support, the man couldn't quite take the leap. Sensing shame would do more than sound advice or round after round of cheerleading, the Count launched a campaign with a single irritating theme: "What does an Irishman know about French food?" After a while, the Irishman had taken all he could stand and opened his own restaurant in the very heart of the French Quarter. In addition to another classy dinner house, New Orleans and the world soon could enjoy a liquor-laced, sauce-happy celebration aimed at starting the day—Breakfast at Brennan's.

The city of Count Arnaud, with its European outlook and life-style, felt few of the moral traumas that afflicted the United States in the early days of this century. The twenties roared elsewhere, but they raised the noise level in Arnaud's already-raucous neighbor-hood nary a decibel.

Even the National Prohibition Act, which curtailed drinking in many cities and sent it into secrecy in the rest, could not quell the sometimes tawdry celebration that passed for everyday life in the town nicknamed Crescent City. The law, which took its ribbing even in the dryest of towns, was the laughingstock of the French Quarter. Its denizens had built too much of their lives around alcohol to replace it under government pressure. And the city, with a tolerance for corruption born of its colorful cosmopolitan roots and a thriv-ing contingent of Mafiosi, found it took only the simplest forms of deception to keep the liquor flowing freely.

A product of his own background and acclimated to the new environment, Count Arnaud wasted little effort questioning the mo-rality of life as he found it, focusing instead on operating within the structure he found. Business ran smoothly, even in the first years of the Great Depression—until federal agents decided to shut Ar-naud's down and send its owner to the penitentiary.

For Arnaud, the most serious legal challenge in the restaurant's history came as no surprise. He had grown accustomed to agents poking about; they had caught him on occasion selling game birds out of season and slapped him with increasingly larger fines. They had even made it plain they wanted to crack his technically illegal liquor sales, fining him a hundred dollars in 1921 and ten dollars in 1926 on related charges. A year after that, federal authorities raided his mansion on Esplanade, carting off bottle after bottle of whiskey stored there since before the war.

In 1931, however, the government decided it had had enough of Arnaud's casual regard for enforced temperance. The ever-frus-trated agents were instructed to build an ironclad case—one, in the words of the Prohibition administrator, "with no possible come-backs."

Applying the sort of technique that matured into sophisticated "sting" operations fifty years later, two agents visited Arnaud's several times in a single ten-day period. Since it was not possible to electronically record these meetings, the government relied on the agents' testimony. Accompanied by a Spanish informer, they posed as a doctor and a visitor from Nicaragua who passionately wanted a drink. In return for tips lavish for the time—up to one dollar—Arnaud's waiters served alcoholic drinks to the agents. One agent even used a rubber syringe to siphon off liquor and carry it away as evidence.

Arnaud was arrested with two of his waiters. Over the next two years, they were indicted on twenty-seven different Prohibition charges, sufficient to padlock the restaurant long enough to snuff out its life and put its high-profile proprietor behind bars. When the case finally came up for trial, after the usual ebb and flow of technicalities, the agents testified not only that Arnaud's waiters had served them liquor illegally but also that the Count himself had joined them for a drink. Jurors, however, perhaps under the influence of the Count's charm or perhaps just weary of the whole affair, failed to agree on a verdict. Arnaud was acquitted.

At last at liberty to run a restaurant again, the Count applied all his energies—and a hefty slice of profits from illegal liquor sales—to expanding his turf at every opportunity, and opportunity knocked regularly in his part of the French Quarter. It was, in spite of Arnaud's more respectable presence, a terrible neighborhood, one in which the pleasures of flesh overshadowed the pleasures of palate. "But," the Count recalled in later years, "the girls in the houses moved away or they died, and as they did, to protect my restaurant, I kept buying up the nearby property. One girl who died —I think she came from Tennessee—I had to take her body down to the railroad station myself."

The land the Count chose for his restaurant came with records dating as far back as 1765, when it was described as two lots forming a corner of Bourbon and Bienville streets and adjoining property owned by Sieur Rennes and Sieur La Rose, where houses stood. The current building was constructed on the site beginning on

February 27, 1883, by Victor Seghers. What eventually became 811–817 Bienville was passed down through the Griffin and Chapotel families between 1888 and 1924, when it was acquired by Dixie Homestead. Count Arnaud purchased the property on October 15, 1924.

In the years that followed, the restaurateur added each adjoining building to his restaurant as soon as it went on the market. Eight-nineteen Bienville, which had remained in the Bock family from the 1830s until 1917, was picked up from Dixie Homestead on February 3, 1927. From Mercer Realty and Investment came a central lot sliced off from 819–823 on February 18, 1936, while from the wife of John Ciolina came 825–829 on September 19, 1946. On the same day and also from Mrs. Ciolina, Arnaud bought 831–833 Bienville—an address that had acquired its only significant publicity in 1885, when it was described in newspaper accounts as a favored hangout of "opium fiends."

As the Count pursued his dream, he wasted little concern on how these very different properties fit together, stylistically or even structurally. They were architecturally of a piece, mixing stucco and brick with plenty of wooden shutters and wrought iron, so whenever Arnaud pulled in a new building, he simply figured out how its floors meshed with the adjoining structure and connected the two by steps, halls, or passageways. In doing so, he built Arnaud's into a tangle of private dining rooms and shadowy storage areas, with more than a few secret spots for liaisons.

As designed by the Count, 811 Bienville welcomed diners through a tiled vestibule, with the main dining room to the right. Comfortable chairs were arranged around tables covered in snowy damask. On the left was the popular Arnaud's Grill, which served as a friendly watering hole for businessmen lacking the time or inclination for a full-course lunch in the dining room. Upstairs waited the web of private dining rooms and a banquet hall capable of seating 250.

In its prime, Arnaud's kitchen was huge, up-to-date, and immaculately kept. The Count insisted that a great restaurant's kitchen be a delicate balance of old and new. The recipes, skills, and attitude had to be true to the Old World, while the equipment and systems had to reflect the very latest developments. The Count was proud of his fine giant kettles of aluminum banded in copper, of his great fifty-gallon stockpot, of his towering stacks of shiny pots and pans. Though few diners ever toured Arnaud's kitchen, the essence of the restaurant's theater was supported by the professionalism behind the scenes.

Though he, as ever, provided the "outline," the Count was even prouder of his succession of chefs than of the equipment they used. When Madame Pierre passed away, he employed Louis Lamothe to direct the kitchen and Jean Laune to serve as his assistant. Both were pupils of the famed Gardère brothers, chefs to Napoléon III. At their deaths, Arnaud discovered Jean Baptiste Lauhle (by sheer coincidence born in Bosdarros) and selected him to succeed Louis and Jean.

The wine cellar remained under the Count's personal supervision until the day he died, reflecting not only infinite care but a master's sophisticated tastes. He selected for his guests the rarest of sauternes, sparkling pink burgundies, and fine Italian chiantis, along with vintages from Alsace and the Moselle and, above all, the champagnes he stocked as his pride and joy—Veuve Cliquot, G.H. Mumms Cordon Rouge, Pol d'Arey, Cliquot Lucien. Perhaps a bit ahead of his time, Arnaud turned his gaze on occasion from traditional Europe to the finest wines made in North and South America.

The Count built Arnaud's reputation during difficult years. The Great Depression was first felt in New Orleans as early as 1930, and within three years no fewer than five of the city's banks had slipped into liquidation and 11 percent of the state's population had gone on relief. Desperation was such that the despotic measures proposed by Huey Long made perfectly good sense. His assault on the Governor's Mansion, the U.S. Senate, and the White House began in Louisiana, and it reached all but the final goal before a bullet ended the Kingfish's climb. Even so, the Depression had its brighter sides, such as the attention focused on New Orleans by writers, actors, and artists of the Works Progress Administration. The city's history, culture, and cuisine took on fresh allure nationwide at the hands of these WPA chroniclers, who even in hard times recognized an intriguing city when they saw one.

Arnaud's struggled on through the Depression, finding its customers among the financial survivors and adjusting its prices to a devastated economy. Some of the Count's most famous cocktails could be had for thirty-five cents—but then, who had thirty-five cents? Money began to loosen up with the start of World War II, especially when the military hierarchy ate and drank its way through New Orleans en route to important maneuvers at Louisiana's Fort Polk. The enlisted troops had to wait a bit longer, many tasting the Count's creations for the first time with bankrolls acquired upon discharge. Even with a new worldliness acquired in European or Pacific theaters, these GIs waxed eloquent over the food and the ambiance.

In his final years, Count Arnaud was forced to reassess his vision of life against the inevitability of death. On his seventieth birthday in 1946, he addressed the issue offhandedly. "It is possibly a fact," said the Count. "But it is my secretary who usually informs me of such things."

But along with his morning champagne, Arnaud mourned the loss of his youth and the opportunity to pursue new ventures. He forced himself instead to concentrate on Arnaud's and its future after he was gone. Lady Irma seemed content enough to take over this legacy, and her parents and brothers had all been restaurateurs. Yet the Count had a major reservation about her—she did not like to drink. After a life in liquor sales, saloon management, and French Quarter restaurant ownership, Arnaud found it impossible to imagine anyone running a successful operation without sharing large amounts of alcohol with guests. So despite a contrasting set of misgivings, he focused his hopes on his only child. Germaine, he realized all too well, liked to drink.

Count Arnaud was told shortly after the end of World War II that he had cancer in both his lungs. He shared this fact with virtually no one, continuing to reign at his restaurant and grace each table with his presence. Yet those who knew him noticed the change as his energy flagged and he grew thinner, as though the larger-than-life aura that surrounded him had been mysteriously but lethally dissolved. As the 1940s wound down, Arnaud spent more and more time at Southern Baptist Hospital, where he was regularly visited and kept abreast by chefs, bartenders, and waiters from his restaurant.

Whenever he felt up to it, the Count continued to visit his

famous dining place. But even then he bowed to the inevitable by seeing only his closest friends and receiving them only in private. In the dining room his absence was felt permanently on May 28, 1948. After a month of hospitalization, Count Arnaud passed away, leaving a $325,000 legacy to his wife but most of his dreams to his daughter. Arnaud's shut down for two days in his memory, then went back to the business of serving food and drink.

A Daughter's Love

$\mathcal{T}$o the world at large, the Count left little doubt as to whom he considered his rightful heir. Shortly before his death, he was asked during a dinner in his honor at New York's Waldorf-Astoria who would take over the restaurant. He answered without hesitation, "My daughter." Yet beneath the surface of this certainty, Arnaud was concerned about the future. He often told his wife and daughter, "You'll never make it go."

Germaine had from a tender age proven herself headstrong and oblivious to any discipline. Despite her father's objections, she exhibited an undying affection for the stage and at least a modicum of talent. While still in her teens, Germaine won a statewide talent contest over 249 rivals and packed her bags to enjoy the grand prize—a cross-country tour on the RKO vaudeville circuit. Thereafter, she was incessantly running away from home for reasons understandable and otherwise—from studying voice and falling in love with a Danish prince in Paris to chasing the Tulane University football team to California for the Rose Bowl. Even when the gun ending the game had sounded, Germaine stayed on in Pasadena. She liked California and remained there for six months but eventually headed home by train.

At the station in shadowy Juarez, someone recognized her from Arnaud's and asked what she was doing there. "I'm going home," she said but immediately sought directions to the bullring. "If you go there," came back the reply, rich with a theatricality Germaine adored, "you'll never go home." On that Mexican afternoon, at least, she chose to do the responsible thing, skipping the *corrida* and catching her train home. Once back in New Orleans, however, her wishes ran as strongly against her father's as ever. She sang locally with the San Carlo Opera, performed regularly with the Little Theater, got married to and divorced from first James Kennell and then Barkeley Wells, and gave birth to a daughter she named Arnaud.

For all the trauma surrounding it, the theater was far from Germaine's most dangerous flirtation. Even her father, no teetotaler on his dryest days, was worried about the way she devoured alcohol. As a young woman, even as a young mother, she made it a regular thing to turn up at Arnaud's between lunch and dinner and raid the liquor supply. Night-shift workers sometimes found her in the bar, sampling the wares with two or three male companions. The abuses became so frightful that the Count handed down one of his strictest orders ever—never, under any circumstances, fix Germaine a drink.

Arnaud's most famous and talented bartender, "Mr. Herman," who held court more than half a century, recalled that the only time the Count fired him was the time he *seemed* to make drinks for Germaine. She had entered the bar with a trio of men, ordered him to serve them cocktails, and became abusive when he refused. "That's all right," she said finally. "I'll come get them myself." The

Count walked in just as Germaine was getting started, turned livid over what he perceived as disobedience, and fired Mr. Herman on the spot. But by the time the bartender had reached the corner, the maitre d' stopped him and said the Count wished him to return.

For all her flightiness, Germaine loved her father deeply and admired him even more. During her formative years, he was the only one who could influence her behavior; Lady Irma had little sway when it came to parental discipline. Undoubtedly Germaine and her father understood each other, and that understanding proved the basis for the restaurant's succession.

Whatever he did for money and however he viewed its attractions, the Count saw theater at the heart of dining out. The drinks had to be fine and strong enough to kick, the food had to be classy and skillfully served, the atmosphere had to be special in sight and sound—yet running a restaurant, he knew from the start, was more than the sum of its parts. It was creating a little bit of magic, weaving a spell around people at a table and lifting their spirits.

When Arnaud's death thrust the weight of the future onto his daughter's shoulders, she had little in the way of personal resources to give her strength or stability. Certainly she had traveled in Europe with her father while he chose wines for the restaurant, but she had slept away the days and swirled away the nights in a flurry of pleasures and learned little. "I loved life," she recalled later. "I loved people and I was young. I really didn't pay too much attention to the restaurant business then."

Within a few months of her father's death, however, Germaine had edged her mother out of the picture and embarked on a crash course that would shape the remainder of her life. She began by studying all the suppliers her father had known through the years, finding out where they were and what they sold. She studied the invoices, sampled the food as it arrived, and even started visiting the locations where it was grown, packed, or processed. The suppliers soon learned she could be as demanding as her father had been.

Confounded by Arnaud's traditional accounting system, Germaine set up her own quirky method of keeping books and signed on an accountant who would do things her way. When a competitor suggested that an exchange of information might prove beneficial to both, she replied, "I'll tell you what, if you won't show me your books, I won't show you mine."

Realizing she had much to learn, Germaine went to Paris and studied cooking, toured the French vineyards to see how wine was made, and became something of an expert. She once rejected an entire order of vintage wine, insisting it came from the wrong town. Germaine traveled north to Chicago, visiting the meatrooms one after another and handpicking seven suppliers. In New York, when another purveyor talked her into trying his meats, she checked over the initial order, found gristle in the steaks, and canceled the contract immediately.

Germaine adopted her father's penchant for new recipes, and whenever a chef argued more than a little, she fired him and went into the kitchen herself. Within a few years, she had added at least half a dozen new selections to the menu—including Hawaiian Ham Steak, made with a white roux, wine, and champagne; Canapés à la Irma, named after her mother and prepared with shrimp and hard-boiled eggs, and Watercress Salad à la Germaine. With her father's memory squarely before her, she added a spectacular new drink called the Germaine Special, made with whiskey, gin, and triple sec, topped with the Count's favorite, champagne, and a twist of orange.

Though seemingly her evenings left her with little energy for early rising, Arnaud's daughter departed strikingly from his time-honored daily routine. Her days at the restaurant could begin as early as 9:00 A.M., which found her dealing with advertising salesmen and handling correspondence with purveyors and diners from around the world. Sharing recipes was alone a major task, as Arnaud's became the darling of the nation's newspapers and magazines. Germaine was usually generous with information about how her specialties were made, though she fibbed on a few favorites and flatly refused on a beloved handful.

Once the lunch crowd was flowing out, she would usually go home to the mansion her father had bought and sleep until it was time for dinner—the second act in what she viewed as a daily dramatic production. She would peek into the kitchen immediately upon her return, then head for the front of the house to serve as official hostess. "I'll bet," she once mused in the presence of foreign ambassadors, "your business isn't as diplomatic as mine."

Unlike her father, Germaine did not make a habit of having a drink at every table before the night was through. After greeting any celebrities and welcoming any old friends, she made it a point (at least in the early years) never to drink with patrons unless she was invited to do so. Her night usually ended at 12:30 A.M., when the restaurant closed its doors.

Though she lived in her father's shadow from the day of her birth, Germaine used the aspect of her personality that most rankled him to spread his fame farther than he had ever dared dream. It was pure theater, she realized, to speak with reporters and give them the message she wanted to get out. And she found in that theater her ultimate role. By the early 1950s, whenever Germaine went anywhere in the world, she was avidly announced and interviewed by the local press. Readers who could not travel to New Orleans found themselves relishing instead the tales she recounted of the city's raucous nightlife and magnificent Creole cuisine.

In August 1950, the New York *Herald Tribune* noted Germaine's arrival in town by describing her as "dark and dynamic, and French to her fingertips." The newspaper chronicled efforts by the Plaza Hotel to prepare Shrimp Creole in a way that met her specifications. A few years later, the *Hong Kong Standard* and the *China Mail* both told their readers Germaine was touring the East in search of recipes and furnishings for her restaurant's new Orient Room. She warmed at once to a dish called Cantonese Corn with Crabmeat, giving reporters the simplest of reasons for taking the dish back. "We have corn," she said, "and we have crabs."

Though most of the press was admiring—Paris's *Journal du Dimanche* described Arnaud's as one of the five best restaurants in the world when Germaine toured the Pyrenees searching for the ultimate *piperade*—some reports were a bit patronizing to this inflated grande dame from the South. The *Chicago Sun-Times* followed her exploits in 1950 when she swirled into town for a restaurant convention, then ignored all the meetings in favor of the city's dining scene. "I'm not interested in learnin' how to run a cafeteria," she drawled to more faithful conventioneers. "When you start discussin' French restaurants, I'll be back."

Perhaps Germaine's single greatest international coup was propelling Arnaud's into a special celebration of Paris's 2,000th birthday at Le Café Chambord in New York in 1951. Chef Jean Pierre was sent to prepare Oysters Bienville, Canapés à la Irma, Filet de Truite Meunière-Amandine, and Suprême de Volaille en Papillote. Arnaud's was joined in the month-long party by only four restaurants from around the world—Romanoff's of Hollywood, the Pump Room of Chicago, Château Frontenac of Quebec, and Maxim's of Paris. "Thus," crowed the menu, "without moving from your favorite table at the Chambord, you can savor successively the spécialités de la maison that have done so much to contribute to the prestige of French cookery."

Germaine demonstrated the greatest respect for traditions her father had built, but she also steered a course faithful to dreams the Count had never brought to life. In his final years, for example, he had spoken lovingly of creating a new bar at Arnaud's—one with an entrance and a life all its own. Though favored patrons seemed to prefer their cocktails in a musty old foyer off the kitchen, there was a quite different clientele strolling nightly along Bienville and, of course, along adjacent Bourbon. The ever-savvy Count longed to accommodate these people in a separate cocktail lounge but died before he could do more than lay the most fundamental groundwork.

Picking up on her father's direction, Germaine returned from a visit to Paris shortly after his death and announced the birth of the Richelieu Bar. Her sense of history was none too deep ("After all," she told reporters, "Richelieu ruled France, didn't he?") but her sense of style was faultless. With its independent foyer leading off Bienville, the bar became an instant success with tourists and especially the local legal establishment—with both sides in many a bitter dispute gleefully rehashing the day's testimony as delivered at the nearby federal courthouse.

By design, the Richelieu looked ancient from the day it opened its doors. It boasted perhaps a dozen stools, with one full mirror gracing the drinkers' backs and another shimmering on the street side. Except for the lacquered mustard-colored plaster, everything was mahogany. There were three chandeliers—clusters of four bare bulbs hanging from ceiling fans. And there were yellowing photos at every turn, showing the Count and his family, Carnival scenes, and, inevitably, Germaine in all her splendor. Over Lady

Irma's strong objections, Germaine hung a portrait of the Cardinal himself in the bar she made his namesake. "He drank just like anyone else, Mother," she argued. "And I like it because he's pointing down at me." With Mr. Herman pouring, the Richelieu Bar was little short of a vision, especially on the "dress-up nights" Germaine modeled after those she had experienced at Maxim's.

During her long life and reign at Arnaud's, Germaine reveled in the city's most famous social tradition, the pre-Lenten bacchanal leading up to Mardi Gras, and taught its populace to love yet another, her ever-quirky Easter Parade. The first celebration was one she had shared with her father; to the second, started several years after his death, she gave a decidedly feminine touch.

New Orleans' world-famous Carnival goes back to primitive celebrations of the coming of spring; later, the Greeks and Romans turned it into something some modern celebrants would applaud —an excuse for debauchery. When the Christian Church came into existence, steps taken to stamp out the practice met with such resistance that it was instead absorbed into church ritual, complete with an overlay of fasting and penance. The Christians called the blowout *carnelevarre,* a Latin term which loosely translated means a "farewell to flesh," or, even more loosely, a last chance to sin.

With elitism Germaine would have appreciated, early Carnival was rich with high-society dances and dramas strung out over several weeks. But with passing time these gave way to a lighthearted street party given a special name by the French. They dubbed the last big orgy Mardi Gras, or Fat Tuesday.

In March 1699, a party of French explorers camped near the mouth of the Mississippi gave in to homesickness and popped open champagne for the first Mardi Gras in America. By the time New Orleans was settled upriver, the observance was no more than a series of drunken street brawls, but by the time the city embarked on its reign as queen of the river, elaborate balls and nightlong dinners served on plates of gold had been added to the annual festivities.

New Orleans picked up on parading in 1837, when a new social group calling itself Mystick Krewe of Comus paid tribute to Milton's *Paradise Lost* with demons and gods marching through the darkened city. From that night forward, Carnival organizations were known as krewes, after the poet's "unholy krewe of demons," spelled with the early English "k."

There was no aspect of Mardi Gras Germaine did not cherish. She especially loved the secrecy and the masking, which freed people from their inhibitions and allowed them to behave virtually as they pleased. There were secret memberships, invitations from secret senders, and even secret Carnival kings. Whatever the state of her own religious faith, the city's noisy countdown to Lent became for Germaine a deliciously ambiguous symbol for all life had to offer.

All the same, Arnaud's only daughter nourished no great love for revelers in the streets, preferring to spend Carnival behind closed doors or to view the public celebration from a balcony flickering with lamplight. She passionately embraced the society side of Carnival, with its round after round of private parties and invitation-only balls. In all, Germaine reigned over twenty-two Carnival balls (more than anyone else in the city's history), beginning with the Krewe of Iris in 1937 and leading up to the Krewe of Sparta in 1968. For each she commissioned a special sparkling gown, sometimes carrying out the event's theme and other times simply radiating elegant illusion. Each gown found a special place in her Mardi Gras memories, and shortly before her death they found a special place in her restaurant's Mardi Gras Museum.

In later years, Germaine proclaimed her affection for each of the krewes she ruled, recalling the theatrical tensions of getting each sequin just right and the exhilaration of dramatic entrances. Yet she insisted her favorite ball of them all was Prometheus in 1938, when she reigned as queen with her father as king. "I have always said that as long as I live, my father will continue to live," Germaine said in a reflective moment. "I am always talking about him, what he did, what he said. We had so many good times together."

After her father's death, Germaine came to believe New Orleans' pre-Lenten bash wasn't enough of a social event to tide her over from winter to spring. As with Carnival, the theme of rebirth appealed to her and she settled on Easter Sunday as its ultimate observance. During a trip to New York in the early 1950s, Germaine was taken with the sight of the city's grandees parading on foot along Fifth Avenue on Easter Sunday. Stage director that she was, she envisioned the entire affair New Orleans–style, complete with horsedrawn carriages and a see-and-be-seen Mass at St. Louis Cathedral.

As she dreamed it up with her fellow grandes dames, the Easter Parade was a charming procession through the French Quarter, beginning at the Arnaud mansion on Esplanade and ending at the cathedral overlooking spring-green Jackson Square. The carriages (and sometimes even the horses) were bedecked with flowers, and the matrons were done up in their finest pastels. As though stepping back from a nearly completed portrait, Germaine conceived a final touch to set her parade apart. She donned one of the largest, most elaborate hats from her extensive collection and instantly became an annual fixture in news pictures distibuted around the world.

Germaine's life was indeed a Carnival and an Easter Parade as well, each big day merging into the next in flurries of planning and preparation. And her restaurant continued to serve as a magnet, not only to the cream of New Orleans' restaurant-going public but to international celebrities ranging from Errol Flynn to Bob Hope, Loretta Young to Shirley MacLaine, Arthur Godfrey to Bette Midler. Yet beneath the surface of this remarkable bit of self-directed theater that was Germaine's life, the sadness and deterioration were evident more and more, edged onward by a series of diverse misfortunes and an ultimate onslaught of tragedy.

In Germaine's final years, she and her restaurant were beset by troubles that even the federally prosecuted Count would have considered extraordinary. Five times between 1952 and 1963, Germaine was the victim of robbery. She was seriously beaten during the final crime, deepening her feeling of vulnerability from any world outside that of her own creation.

In the 1952 robbery, a knife-wielding bandit took $36,000 worth of diamond rings from her fingers as she returned home after a night at the restaurant. The man held the knife to her throat as she struggled to remove the rings and a bracelet, but left her unhurt. Among the rings taken was a 47.76-carat diamond proclaimed larger than the one called Hope.

In 1953, $20,000 was stolen from an armoire in the hallway of

Germaine's home, and in 1959 a pair of diamond-studded earrings and $2,000 were taken from the apartment she maintained above Arnaud's. The largest of the crimes occurred later the same year, when $125,000 in cash and jewels was stolen from a safe Germaine kept in an unused bedroom of her home.

In 1963, Germaine accepted into her Bienville Street apartment two men who seemed much like dozens she had entertained before. They said they were reporters from New York and wished to interview her for a story about the restaurant. Once inside, however, the pair beat Germaine until she gave them $60,000 in jewels, and tied her up, along with her twenty-one-year-old daughter, Arnaud Milner.

If the law was absent from this series of terrifying encounters, it seemed omnipresent in Germaine's restaurant affairs. A string of damage suits from diners claiming they were somehow wronged kept the proprietor and her lawyers in and out of courts for years. The most publicized of these cases involved a man who claimed he suffered severe internal injuries after swallowing a piece of crabshell. Making its three-year trip through the legal process, the squabble ended up before no less a panel than the 5th U.S. Circuit Court of Appeals, which let stand a $45,000 judgment—all because of a single serving of Pompano en Papillote.

The arrival of the 1960s brought two issues to the fore at Arnaud's that reflected their times, to be sure, but also pushed the frustration level higher than an aging Germaine could tolerate. In one controversy, Arnaud's was slapped with a much-reported civil rights suit by a black dentist refused service along with seven of his well-dressed friends. The other controversy left a much deeper scar. In 1963, up to 95 percent of Arnaud's employees stalked off the job on instructions from their union, an arm of the AFL-CIO. The workers, including cooks, waiters, busboys, bartenders, and porters, were demanding pay raises from 50 to 100 percent, but Germaine insisted that salaries were already substantial and the union demands unreasonable. The walkout was settled after many an angry argument and the union was eventually defeated, but it was already too late for the old Arnaud's. Some insiders, in fact, date the start of the restaurant's slide from this divisive labor dispute. Indeed, many of its most talented workers departed before, during, or shortly after the strike.

Few diners knew or cared, of course, about the succession of blows that drove Germaine deeper into alcoholism and an ultimate retreat from reality. Tourists were largely unaware, and even the locals preferred the vision of Germaine that she herself chose. Ever eccentric. Ever fun-loving. Ever ready for a ball or parade. Yet more and more, the restaurant came to mirror Germaine's sad and steady descent.

By the early 1970s, Arnaud's was a restaurant of dubious renown everywhere but in Germaine's imagination. Despite her stubborn belief that the spirit and perfection of the Count lived on— and would continue under her daughter and then her grandson— the restaurant was a weary relic that snared only the least aware of visitors. The weddings and christenings went elsewhere, as did the celebrities. Germaine, when she was able and sometimes when she was not, still held court in the dining room. But the place seemed empty and broken, with but a waiter and a cook to tide it through some nights. Diners on occasion found the restaurant closed, with an incredible "Back in a Little While" note tacked to its doors.

The final assault on Germaine's illusion came in 1977. After years of being viewed as Arnaud's heir apparent, Germaine's divorced daughter died suddenly and somewhat mysteriously, leaving her with a young grandson. Even in her condition, Germaine could see the horrendous odds against her working long enough for Arnaud Milner to take over.

In a personal sense, Germaine chose retreat, the sort that would intrigue many a playwright. What once were baubles of her restaurant career—the sequined gowns, the flowery hats—became the stuff of life itself. Certainly her city cherished eccentrics, and certainly it cherished Germaine. Yet it made clear on a daily basis that its affection stopped short of patronizing her restaurant.

To sad-eyed chroniclers of New Orleans society, the news in 1978 had all the trappings of final surrender. Germaine was leasing her father's legacy to a little-known hotel man named Archie Casbarian, who didn't even come from the city. Predictions leaned heavily toward the bleak, especially among Germaine's dwindling circle of friends. But Germaine's single toughest decision would prove a brilliant one.

The lady's final ceremonial turn came in late 1983, after her controversial choice had resurrected Arnaud's and even enshrined her beloved gowns in the city's only Mardi Gras Museum. Germaine arrived for the museum's opening in the gold lamé she'd worn as Queen of Naiads, a sparkling crown atop her coal-black hair, a scepter in her hand. With one last burst of theater, she asked Archie to give her his arm and lead her around the room. This he did, halting whenever she needed to bow or wave, as though their very steps had been set down a century before. Even onlookers given to cynicism found the slow circle touching. And the more they knew of Germaine's life and labors, the more they felt the tribute was deserved.

Germaine Cazenave Wells died in her father's mansion on December 15, 1983. She had known just one other home in all the years of her life, and she was taken past it a final time as the funeral cortege saluted Arnaud's. She was buried in Metairie Cemetery— wearing, at her request, her gold lamé Carnival gown.

A Legend Lives Again

$\mathcal{I}$f one approaches life's turning points with a touch of pure mysticism, as Germaine Wells did from time to time, the arrival of Archie Casbarian at her doorstep must have seemed inevitable. Seen as a simple sequence of choices, however, few arrivals could have appeared less likely.

In a city whose landmarks are as closely held as its secrets, long-time acquaintances wondered how Germaine could have settled on this outsider and, indeed, how she could trust him with her father's legacy. Even on its last legs, Arnaud's seemed a priceless part of New Orleans lore, one that demanded the care and pampering that could only be expected from a native. Yet the truth is that Germaine was approached by quite a few such candidates, including members of several prominent restaurant families. Each had a plan to save Arnaud's, and each in turn Germaine heard out and sent packing; in private she expressed the fear they were more enamored of their own lineage than hers. As the notion of leasing the restaurant took hold of Germaine, it seemed more and more important to her that the person taking over should be free of traditions that might twist his interests and decisions.

Still, the prospect of letting go terrified Germaine. At times, even with her daughter gone, she fantasized about somehow keeping the old place going until her grandson was old enough to replace her. Many another culinary landmark had survived difficult transitions, she told herself, many another had struggled to bridge a painful generation gap. Yet by the time an Egyptian-born hotelier presented her with his proposal to resurrect a restaurant whose greatness he had come too late to experience, even Germaine was all too aware that time was running out.

The grand old lady listened carefully as Archie Casbarian led her through his plans for Arnaud's—restoring it room by tumble-down room, returning its menu to the grandeur of the days when the Count still greeted each guest. She was impressed with his youth, his globe-trotting experience, and his growing reverence for a tradition she was certain deserved nothing less. And she was reassured by his understanding of restaurants as pure theater, an approach Casbarian shared with both Germaine and her father.

Finally, Germaine was pushed past her reticence by a striking (if perhaps meaningless) set of coincidences. Ever the adoring daughter, she saw in Archie a man her father's height, similarly foreign-born, fluent in French, and adept in handling pleasures from liquor to cigars. Even Archie's initials, she realized, matched those of Arnaud Cazenave, making her certain that fate in some way had delivered this man at the precise moment she needed him most.

In December of 1978, Germaine Wells leased out the building that once housed one of the world's great restaurants, setting in motion a $2.5 million restoration that would amaze cynics and rewrite the dining guides that had dropped Arnaud's from listings years before.

Though Germaine no doubt exaggerated the destiny involved in her choice and his, there was in fact a thread in Casbarian's life that made this deal make sense. Arshag Armenag Casbarian grew up far from the Count's Bosdarros, France, but in one of the few cities to rival New Orleans for ethnic entanglements and sheer romantic intrigue. The Alexandria of Archie's childhood was a swirling kaleidoscope of nationalities, cuisines, religions, and sexual preferences, all coexisting on good days and bad with a surprising degree of tolerance. Egyptians formed the majority, of course, but under King Farouk, emigrated Jews, Italians, Maltese, British, Greeks, and Armenians supported themselves in carefully delineated trades.

Armenians such as Archie's father primarily found work selling photo equipment, carpets, and jewelry—products they perceived as being at the artistic ends of commerce. The Casbarians had made their way to Egypt after fleeing persecution elsewhere, including the infamous massacres by the Turks in the early twentieth century. As the son of a district manager for Kodak, Archie grew up with far more comfort and education than was common in his land, including the physical expression of short pants, red and black ties, and beanies required by Alexandria's elite British school system.

Though he remembers the city with affection, increasing racial and religious tensions changed his life dramatically at a time that crucial decisions had to be made. With the deposal of King Farouk and the rise to power of Gamal Abdel Nasser, life for non-Egyptians and non-Moslems became a cat-and-mouse game of abuse, arrest, and sudden violence. Casbarian was seventeen when his parents sent him to Lausanne, Switzerland, for enrollment in the grueling École Hôtelière de la Société Suisse des Hôteliers. On his first two trips back to Alexandria, he found rioting in the streets. On his third, his father told him not to return.

Casbarian *did* return to Egypt, finding his first job at the nationalized Continental Savoy in Cairo. He worked not only to succeed but to bolster his faith in a country on the brink, a faith that squirmed under military oppression and finally was abandoned after his father's arrest. It took the Casbarians more than a year, and great expense, to win the elder Casbarian a presidential pardon. He emerged from his ordeal convinced his son should not only leave Egypt but seek his future in the United States.

Archie Casbarian found it easiest to enter the country as a student and signed up for the rigorous hotel program at Cornell University in Ithaca, New York. If the Swiss diploma opened doors in Europe, Cornell did the same in America—funneling its graduates with regularity into huge hotel chains, some with holdings overseas. That at first was Archie's plan, to return to Europe or even to Egypt with American citizenship his employers would help him acquire. It was not, however, how things developed.

Archie's ascent in the hotel world was rapid, and it did indeed lead to U.S. citizenship. But it also led to New Orleans, with significant stops in Los Angeles, Curaçao, New York, Washington, and Boston along the way. Like Count Arnaud half a century earlier, Archie fell in love with the city. Its climate and life-style reminded him of Alexandria; its European flair disclosed sophistication at every turn and demanded nothing less from him. He was especially impressed by the number of people who invited him into their homes; always, in other cities, he'd been entertained in lounges and restaurants. His fate was clear early on in New Orleans, and it was sealed by his marriage to a local girl named Jane.

Archie was running the Royal Sonesta in the French Quarter when he first started thinking about Arnaud's. Already, in his work as hotel manager, he had heard dozens of locals and visitors recall their great meals there in the years of the Count. The place, he realized, held some special magic, as though it were much more to New Orleans than a building, a kitchen, a collection of tables and chairs. Archie saw the restaurant's potential, and he saw his own as well. Hotel careers by their nature are transient. His prospects for wealth and influence were great, but they certainly threatened his serenity in the French Quarter and his life there with his growing family. Arnaud's would be a step off the corporate treadmill onto a piece of New Orleans history and something he could call his own.

One bit of business remained, however, before Casbarian could settle in. Even after he and two brothers had embarked on careers in the United States, their parents remained in the Middle

East—no longer in Alexandria but in a Beirut becoming less idyllic by the hour. Pulling strings he'd acquired in the hotel business, Archie finally overcame his parents' objections to starting a new life and the U.S. bureaucracy's objections to letting them. He set up a little shop for them in the French Quarter and ultimately invited them into his Arnaud's operation, placing his father in charge of purchasing and his mother in charge of housekeeping. The family business became even more close-knit when Jane Casbarian took up the challenge of the marketing department, eventually helping to design and run the restaurant's popular boutique and becoming hostess of the new Arnaud's.

Such a restaurant, however, was still more dream than reality at the time the lease was signed. And the cost grew more staggering with each adjustment or delay. It was fortunate that Archie kept a firm grip on his vision, refined during two years of research and negotiation. At every opportunity, he had questioned people about Arnaud's—what it looked like, what it felt like, what they remembered about their meal. He also pored over the few surviving documents, including a mere handful of weathered menus and land acquisition histories in the Historic New Orleans Collection. For an entrepreneur with expertise and intuition, the message amidst the malaise was clear: turn back the clock in every way visible yet create a modern, efficient, profitable operation behind the scenes.

"When I was speaking with people about Arnaud's, they always talked about when the Count was alive," Archie remembered. "The perception of the public was that the Count's era was the greatest. So I sought to re-create that era in everything from tuxedos on the waiters to lighting in the dining room—all those elements, every element. You come here to dine, rather than just to eat."

If most of Casbarian's time went into planning the cuisine and atmosphere of Arnaud's, most of his money went into reclaiming its physical structure. Little more than the main dining room was open to the public by the time he took over; the labyrinth of rooms the Count had acquired had long since been shut up. Even the dining room had suffered through a series of "improvements" over the years, in addition to a frightening degree of neglect. It was in the entranceway and the main room that Archie worked out the fine points of his restoration. Closing down Arnaud's for a mere three months, he turned a shadowy barn with pigeons in its upper rooms into a glittering showplace he was confident the Count himself would have admired.

The main dining room got the most dramatically fresh look of all. In addition to the grit and grime of recent abuse, the space suffered from a near-absence of natural light—daylight had to fight its way in through small, dirty panes of milk glass. Archie made the windows larger and brighter, giving a special sunlight shimmer to the business lunches and jazz brunches he introduced. Casbarian also restored the Count's fluted metal columns, which had been covered over with plywood, and removed the fake arches and ceiling latticework, which had concealed many other graceful touches.

The plywood came down from everywhere, the floor was fixed, and the antiquated cashier's cage was banished out of sight. From a dark, distinctly cavelike dining space, the main room took on the brightness of crystal. It was a jewel box now, one New Orleanians and visitors alike would love from the moment they stepped inside.

Arnaud's bars were a special challenge for Archie, since the Richelieu had been for walk-in business while those enjoying pre-dinner cocktails still preferred that scruffy place just off the old kitchen. The notion of two bars appealed to the new proprietor. He made the Richelieu the diners' bar, adding a tin ceiling to replicate the one in the dining room and stripping coats of dirty nondescript paint off stretches of grand old mahogany. Even the old church pews which Arnaud had acquired, and which, according to legend, were sanctuaries for revelers too drunk to sit on stools, were left in place.

For his public bar, Casbarian chose a small dining area called the Men's Grill, complete with fake arches and an unattractive service area. This he resurrected as the Grill Room Bar, outfitted with a mahogany bar from the 1800s and covered with period wallpaper and vintage political cartoons. In a short time, the Grill Room Bar became a favorite of the legal and business communities, just as the Richelieu once had been.

Beyond these newly brightened public areas, Arnaud's twisted on up and down, a jungle of shadows and surprises that revealed its background as a blockful of separate buildings. Yet to accurately reflect the Count's restaurant (and generate the numbers needed for profit), these spaces were essential. With flashlight, camera, and notebook in hand, Archie and Jane poked through these rooms one by one, peering through cobwebs and accumulated mildew, wondering what to do. But by the time Arnaud's was truly back on its feet, these old rooms attracted some of the most extravagant compliments of all.

The new proprietor quickly realized his out-of-town customers might appreciate at least two more elements in their dining experience—a way to take home more than memories and a place to pay tribute to the Cazenaves. Archie added the Arnaud's Boutique, stocking it not only with a growing list of classy restaurant souvenirs (official aprons, chef's hats, even neckties) but also with a careful selection of local gourmet items (led off by Louisiana red beans). Later still, he pumped $25,000 into the city's only Mardi Gras museum, naming it after Germaine, filling it with her Carnival costumes, and opening it to the public free of admission. Here, amidst the sequins and silk of half-forgotten reigns, visitors can find the beam of light that illuminates one incredible lady and the quirky but magnificent city she claimed as her own.

Archie reworked Arnaud's kitchen extensively, bringing it back to the Count's original concept—using the latest equipment to produce classic cuisine. A computerized ordering system organized all cooking, reducing the time a completed dish sat waiting to be served, while special pagers kept inside the waiters' breast pockets enabled them to care for their customers instead of having to check constantly on the next course. This technology proved a major step back toward grandeur, especially among diners who demanded food served at proper temperatures.

The issue of formality was a potentially sticky one. A certain style was necessary to make the magic work, yet many diners in the late twentieth century had little patience with the formality their fathers and grandfathers demanded. Working through the dining experience as if through a series of border checkpoints, Archie found a charming chemistry that blends formality with friendliness. The hostess's introduction of waiters to guests gives them a sense of being insiders, without the false familiarity of the server-as-new-best-friend scenario of "Hi, I'm Chuck and I'll be your waiter this evening."

Archie settled on one waiter per table (four tables to a waiter), eliminating the overblown ceremony and, in our times, the awesome expense of an ever-scurrying army. And he found in his training at the Swiss hotel school a basic tone for the waiter's approach, warmly attentive yet respectful of the diner's privacy.

For all the physical deterioration of its darkest days, Arnaud's food was its most obvious and most serious descent. Inconsistency had driven off local patrons, even the most nostalgic old-timers, and had sparked a wariness among the uninitiated. Archie realized that all the décor in the world couldn't attract and keep diners unless his food was consistently wonderful. It had to reflect and celebrate the Count but fit contemporary style as well.

The first step toward a loving re-creation of Arnaud's menu was well on its way before Archie decided to sign the lease. In conversations with a wide array of former diners, dish after dish and touch after touch came forth as essential to the old sorcery. Some, of course, were simply imagined, the product of lost youth or remembered wine. Others were absolutely accurate but doomed to rejection in a modern restaurant. These included impractical items like Crabmeat Diablo (the crab-shaped glass dishes kept breaking) and antiquated appetizers like stuffed celery and "Imported Sardines." The rest of the memories, imprecise and personal as they were, Archie carried with him on his next serious piece of research—tracking down and going over as many of Arnaud's menus as he could find.

To his dismay and disappointment, only eight original menus turned up, with the earliest traced to 1937. This seemed a terrible loss for a restaurant founded in 1918, but it was the reality and Archie chose to wrestle with it. Besides, most of the memories he had collected centered on the late 1930s, identifying those years as the restaurant's heyday.

Beyond the deceptively low prices of the Great Depression (85 cents for broiled lobster, $1.50 for filet mignon), the new proprietor was struck by a cooking system classic in approach, admirable in execution, but out of touch with today's restaurant business. On the one hand, there seemed too many dishes, as evidenced by the row upon row of fine print in the menu. On the other hand, the variety was a bit misleading in that each of a few basic food items was offered with a numbing selection of sauces and presentations. In any case, executing such a menu, which was not uncommon through the 1950s, is too labor-intensive to make any economic sense today.

Chicken, for instance, was served thirty-three different ways, from sautéed with asparagus or en papillote to made into patties or cooked with spaghetti. Beef turned up forty-one different ways, including a hamburger steak priced at 70 cents—and most of the sauces were the same as for chicken. Most important, despite all the local seafood and produce on the menu, it was clear that the Count had not by 1937 developed the dishes that in time made him famous.

Moving slowly and carefully through the menus printed on thick, richly textured paper, Archie watched as Arnaud made his mark. A menu dating to around 1940 seemed a universe removed from the earlier, with a move under way to reduce the number of dishes and customize their presentations. There were also forty-four dishes printed in red and identified as Arnaud's creations, led off by Shrimp Arnaud and rounded out by a dessert called Monts d'Amour, Rosalinde.

The next handful of menus showed Germaine's attempts to modernize the restaurant according to her own lights. They introduced several of her most famous creations and also spread out the offerings in a more appealing manner, simple black letters on white paper, with specialties and categories singled out in red. By the latest menu Archie uncovered, all the grand old dishes were in place, including the Cantonese Corn Soup with Crabmeat Germaine had tracked down in China. But by then, of course, the restaurant was faltering badly and only a few of these dishes were available on any given night. By the end, at many a mealtime, Shrimp Arnaud and Trout Amandine were the only real choices. The single waiter in sight would promote them so the single cook in the kitchen could handle the order.

Casbarian had to determine just what survived beyond mere words on a printed page, as he reviewed the notebook of recipes that came with the lease. Most of the nuances of each dish, it turned out, had vanished with the chef who prepared it. By working painstakingly through each possible ingredient and combination, recipes were restored to their most spectcular and most consistent form.

As for which dishes stayed and which disappeared, the new proprietor was left with a bit of information, a bit of intuition, and great empty spaces to cross in a hurry. Casbarian drew up his first menu on wishful thinking alone, then hired a kitchen engineer to weed out what could not be done. Several chefs skilled at opening new hotels were brought in for a time, helping with the fine points of menu balance and dish presentation. Casbarian represented the Count's interest throughout, reining in countless inspirations that seemed to conflict with the spirit of Arnaud's.

Virtually every dish people remembered fondly survived this dizzying and highly critical test. Many, in fact, were undoubtedly better than ever before. Shrimp Arnaud led off Archie's menu, still emblazoned proudly in red. Almost all the old Creole soups were there—turtle, oysters stewed in cream, gumbo—along with Oysters Bienville, Rockefeller, and Suzette. The seafood, fowl, and meat selections were faithful versions of Arnaud's tradition yet tended more toward popular grilling and steered clear of most heavy sauces. Among the desserts, bread pudding and crème brûlée stood out most dramatically, ready and waiting to be declared the best anywhere in New Orleans.

Casbarian again found himself working with Count Arnaud in mind as he resurrected the restaurant's once-fabled wine cellar. Arnaud had, after all, been a wine merchant before taking on a Bourbon Street bar and finally a Creole dining palace, so he knew the best and sought it out for his patrons. He even dug an underground cellar—no small task in a city built on sometimes very swampy soil. Casbarian embraced the long-term challenge of returning Arnaud's cellar to greatness, handpicking his wines with a care and sophistication the Count would have applauded. In late 1986, he added a special Proprietor's List, its distinguished selections including seven Château Lafite Rothschilds from 1953 to 1979.

"Tonight," wrote Archie in his inaugural menu for February 28, 1979, "marks the rebirth of a grand and noble restaurant and heralds a new era in the history of a world-famous establishment."

Those fortunate enough to attend that festive dinner were served Shrimp Arnaud, Oysters Stewed in Cream, Pompano en Croûte, Filet Charlemond, Potatoes Soufflé, String Beans Sauté, Spinach Salad Louis, Pineapple and Louisiana Yams Flambé à la Germaine, and, of course, Arnaud's renowned Café Brûlot.

An auspicious beginning, to be sure, yet the hard work was far from over. There was still a skeptical city to conquer, and a skeptical world beyond that. Besides the predictable efforts to improve and promote the fact, three other events thrust Arnaud's back into the international spotlight.

One was the opening of the Mardi Gras Museum, which drew attention from newspapers across the country. Any story, it seemed, linking New Orleans with its famous street party was news in cities more sedate. The second boost came unexpectedly, when Folger's chose Arnaud's as one of "the world's great restaurants" and filmed a commercial in its dining room. The TV spot ran and ran, making Arnaud's a household name to a new generation thousands of miles from the French Quarter. Among visitors to the city, the impact of the commercial was immense.

Arnaud's third breakthrough was the quirkiest of all. In search of cash for his ongoing renovation, Archie hit on the notion of "selling" certain tables for $10,000 each. In truth, it was more like signing a three-year lease, with $12,000 in food credit attached, but the idea of ownership caught on immediately. The wire services fired the story around the world, sparking a month or more of live interviews by far-flung radio stations and an extended segment on NBC's "Today" show. All ten tables were sold, and Casbarian went on with his renovation. And Arnaud's had received millions of dollars' worth of publicity.

Suddenly, it seemed, the restaurant was a must again, a magnet for every visiting food writer, a mandatory part of every food article written about the city. Medals and ribbons again covered its walls, and stars, diamonds, forks, toques, and other culinary rating symbols again accompanied the slightest mention in print. The restaurant was back in a global spotlight. And best of all, after years of work by dozens of professionals and plenty of love from the Casbarians, it was ready.

At 10 P.M. on the last day of 1986, Archie and business partner

Ralph O'Connor of Houston finalized the purchase of all Arnaud's properties from heirs of the Count and Germaine. The acquisition was especially satisfying to Archie, since it confirmed at last on paper what had long been true in spirit—the new Arnaud's was indeed his.

Creole and Cajun Cuisines

*T*hough cuisines are often born in strange and wondrous ways, it is doubtful that any other than Creole got its start because housewives threatened a governor with cast-iron pots and pans. In 1722, in what became known as the "Petticoat Rebellion," about fifty young wives marched on Governor Bienville's mansion in New Orleans, pounding their frying pans with metal spoons and protesting their dreary diet of cornmeal mush.

With a dash of admirable dexterity, Bienville put the women in touch with his own housekeeper, a certain Madame Langlois, who had learned more than a few secrets from the local Choctaw

Indians. It was she who calmed the angry wives by teaching them
how to use powdered sassafras for flavor in gumbo, how to make
hominy grits, how to get the most from the region's abundant fish
and game. From this education, a tempering of French tradition
with Indian pragmatism, Creole cooking was born.

Ever since the bizarre beginning, and probably even before,
two things have been clear about the Creoles. The first is that no
two people agree on who or what they are. The second, fortunately,
is that everyone agrees they really know how to cook.

By some definitions, virtually everyone in New Orleans seems
to be a Creole. By others, there's hardly anyone who measures up.
According to most dictionaries, Creole comes from the same Latin
root as the word "create," with the French creating their *creole*
from the Spanish *criollo*. Over time, this went from denoting a
person born of Spanish parents overseas to a person born similarly
of French parents. A child of the colonies, in either case. Yet Creole
can also mean a mix of black and white parentage, or even undi-
luted black. It's undeniable that much of the sweat and soul that
went into Creole food came from the black women who ran every
home kitchen and the black men who labored in every professional
one.

Despite a Creole passion for bloodlines, generations of alli-
ances legal and otherwise added more tangles to the web that
produced their cuisine. To French, Spanish, and African roots, suc-
cessive waves of immigrants contributed fascinating touches from
Italy, Germany, even Yugoslavia. The Cajuns, a distinct French-
speaking group living along the bayous, brought a love of hot peppers—though they never pushed Creole cooking dramatically in
that direction. After all these years, the result is a cuisine that looks
French in sophistication yet packs more punch and, on any table,
carries more surprises.

Today, Creole is as different from Cajun as city is from country
—with each boasting its own delights and its own enthusiastic par-
tisans. Cajun cuisine (at least the real Cajun food, before the onset
of chic) is home cooking at its finest, usually requiring large
amounts of time and love to make up for missing expenditure.
Creole cuisine, as showcased at Arnaud's, is the city cooking of New

Orleans, much closer than Cajun is to the classic techniques of Paris and much more likely to involve an eye-catching degree of theater.

What follows is part glossary, part travel guide, and part collection of helpful hints. It covers the most famous Creole creations and the main ingredients, vegetables, and flavorings used to prepare them. Most of these elements come into play at Arnaud's every lunch and dinner, dressed up a bit to suit the restaurant's style yet true to the home kitchens that first laid down the law.

The Basics

$\mathcal{R}$ *oux* Traditional French chefs thought they knew what was what when it came to making a roux. They named this thickener, after all, defining it as flour browned with butter or other fat. But then they flung it to the peasantry in favor of the classic brown sauce. The thinking around New Orleans is that the peasants got the better part of that deal.

Once perfected by the black cooks in the city and the Cajuns along the bayou, the roux became a thing of beauty, adding a deep, resonant flavor to seafood, game, and vegetables. The renowned Escoffier declared a roux indigestible the instant it turned dark brown, and there remain a handful of Creoles who agree. Most, however, prefer a roux that's as dark as you can get it without scorching.

Making your own perfect roux is time-consuming, to be sure. But on any scale of culinary skills, it can't be rated among the most difficult. Just melt butter in a heavy skillet over low heat, then add an equal measure of flour. Once the mixture is stirred free of lumps, increase the heat to medium and stir calmly but constantly for as long as it takes to brown.

Nonstop scraping will keep the roux from sticking to the pan and burning, until it's precisely the color you want. Then you can set it aside for use as you see fit, or even for freezing in small individual packets.

R ice The average Creole would give the average Chinese a run for his money in rice consumption. And he has little patience for such exotic varieties as basmati or risotto. Rice is that white stuff harvested all around him in Louisiana, then cooked with an amazing degree of care. Proportionate to its popularity, the respect given rice in Creole and Cajun cuisines sets it apart from the often gummy mounds carrying the name farther north. Every grain is completely cooked, but it's also separate and dry.

Most traditional Creole cooks boil rice in plenty of slightly salted water, until it feels right to the teeth—achieves a pleasant texture. The rice not to use is "instant," which the Creoles, like other serious cooks, insist is an inferior product and takes just about as long as ordinary rice anyway.

G umbo It's said that duels have been fought over which kind of gumbo is really the best—okra or filé. Of course, around New Orleans, duels have been fought over a lot of things. Suffice it to say that in Creole country, gumbo is the ultimate soup. It also carries a tangled pedigree that goes back to the farmer's pot-au-feu and fisherman's bouillabaisse in France, to tribal stews in pre-slavery Africa, and to Indian boiled seafood in pre-Colonial Louisiana.

Like virtually any great stew, gumbo can be made with just about anything—and good times or bad, it already has been. Chicken or turkey work well with the spicy sausage called *andouille,* while duck and squirrel turn up regularly during hunting season. During Lent, the Catholics of New Orleans are likely to serve gumbo z'herbes, in which meat is displaced by seven types of greens. Still, whether okra or filé is chosen as thickener, the seafood gumbo of New Orleans has to take a special place in every soup-lover's pantheon. It usually features shrimp, oysters, and crabs (either picked out or still in the shell). Once the roux is successfully browned and the thickening agent is picked, preferably without estrangement or bloodshed, Creole gumbo is a matter of delightful self-expression.

É touffée   The Cajuns traditionally kept to themselves, their main encounter with English-speaking people having been their exile by the British from Nova Scotia. Yet they did contribute many a touch to classic Creole cooking, sometimes a pinch of this or that and sometimes an entire dish. Étouffée, usually prepared with crawfish or shrimp, is one of the latter contributions. The name means nothing more than "smothered," but the tastes and textures are much more interesting than the name. In fact, the Creoles love étouffée so much they often claim it as one of their own creations. In étouffée, such vegetables as chopped green pepper, onion, and celery are cooked in a roux until opaque, then joined by the crawfish or shrimp and a bit of liquid; the mixture is then cooked until the seafood is tender.

Jambalaya   No visit with the Creoles or Cajuns would be complete without at least one serving of jambalaya; and no visitor could find much within a day's drive that hasn't turned up in this famous dish. According to language experts, the name is derived from the Spanish word for ham, *jamon,* a regular ingredient in the eighteenth century. New Orleanians, however, love to defy language experts right along with everybody else.

Jambalaya, they insist, got its name when a gentleman stopped at an inn too late to find anything to eat. The cook, whose name happened to be Jean, was directed to "mix some things together" —an order that came out *"Balayez."* The guest loved the concoction that came his way, dubbing it "Jean Balayez" in tribute. Or so goes the story. The present spelling originated, it seems, with *The Picayune's Creole Cook Book* of 1872, describing a "Spanish-Creole" dish that could be made with beef, pork, chicken, shrimp, oysters, crawfish, or virtually anything else. The passion continues to this day, with the city of Gonzales, outside New Orleans, declaring itself the Jambalaya Capital of the World and hosting an annual festival devoted to the dish's enjoyment.

Bisque   This is another of those New Orleans dishes that can embody the best of peasant food or the finest in haute cuisine, depending on just who is making it. Its French origins are fairly ancient and mysterious, with some authorities pointing to a half-forgotten purée of wood pigeons, other poultry, and game. Other researchers, however, have traced the word "bisque" to a shellfish soup of Provence. That, at any rate, is the root of the thick delicacy Creoles and Cajuns love today.

In the French-speaking countryside of south Louisiana, bisque most often was prepared with crawfish—including the crustaceans' bright red heads, cleaned out and stuffed with seasoned tailmeat. In the Creole city, the soup most often was a thick and creamy concoction of crab or shrimp. At its most sophisticated, bisque becomes the sort of setting in which you find lobster; and indeed, in other parts of the country, you often do.

Rémoulade The word comes from the Picard dialect of France, where *ramolas* means simply horse-radish. Actually, there are at least three versions of rémoulade sauce likely to turn up in the culinary world—two on a regular basis. The French still prefer a mayonnaise dressing or sauce, which carries the name in the most classical sense. The Creoles turned that recipe on its ear, making it an attack on the sinuses with horseradish or Dijon mustard, and sometimes adding crumbled hard-boiled eggs. Finally, a green rémoulade, or *rémoulade verte,* is either of the above with chopped parsley added. For the record, the Creoles took off from the French for their sauce and Count Arnaud took off from them both. His recipe for the rémoulade-based Arnaud Sauce, used to dress his famous shrimp, remains a secret.

Beignets To natives of New Orleans, there's no such thing as a meal too huge to top off with fresh beignets at a sidewalk café in the French Quarter. These air-light yeast pastries are deep-fried in oil so hot they puff out in surprise, then covered with blizzards of powdered sugar.

Pronounced "ben-yays" (no matter what the tourists call them), they are the predestined and perfect sidekick for rich café au lait. An order of three is standard for each celebrant, under any circumstances. In recent years, some of the more imaginative New Orleans chefs have taken to putting things like crawfish, duck, or rabbit into their dough, and eliminating the sugar, to create savory beignets. These are reminiscent of the really light conch fritters found along the Florida Keys or the Bahamas. There are certainly those who find such experimentation abhorrent, preferring the sweet, light pastries they remember from childhood.

Coffee The Creoles, like the French who gave them their language, had a word for it. And when it came to coffee, they had several words. They described their perfect coffee as *"Noir comme le diable, fort comme la mort, doux comme l'amour, et chaud comme l'enfer."* Coffee, to the old Creoles, had to be black as the devil, strong as death, sweet as love—and hot as hell.

They opened their eyes to strong, sweet coffee and only later breakfasted with cup after cup of café au lait. Café noir remained the standard for consumption throughout the day, its flavor tinged with pleasantly bitter chicory, while the mixture of coffee and scalded milk helped set off Creole desserts from bread pudding to Bananas Foster. Café au lait also became the perfect accompaniment to hot, sugar-sifted beignets, preferably enjoyed out of doors with sun and cool breeze finding paths through the awnings. Before long, however, the words of chroniclers from the north settled on café brûlot as the ultimate Creole brew. This blazing combination of coffee, brandy, Grand Marnier, cinnamon, cloves, orange, and lemon peel proved a memorable marriage of taste with dazzling theater.

The Main Ingredients

$\mathscr{C}$ *rawfish*   There was a time when northerners pronounced it "crayfish" just to make Creoles and Cajuns mad, and they tirelessly mocked the entire notion that these tiny "mud-bugs" were edible. The French have always known better. And finally, so does just about everybody else. In fact, tons of crawfish a year stream off to parts unknown—places like New York and Paris. At the very least, this newfound international chic keeps prices at roadside crawfish stands from plummeting so low at season's height that the locals live on nothing but.

All the same, diners can almost always find this delicacy at

Arnaud's, showcased in creations ranging from spicy Crawfish Bourgeois to sophisticated Crawfish Wellington. In the kitchen, crawfish tails are the ingredients most often called for, so finding them fresh or frozen is the quickest means to an end. Live crawfish are a bit more trouble, since they must be boiled to a lovely red before their meat can be picked out. Investing this labor, however, entitles the crawfish lover not only to the tailmeat but also to the fat so beloved of Louisiana cooks for the flavor it imparts.

Shrimp   This is America's favorite seafood, with a distinctive taste and tender, juicy meat. Shrimp present the Creole cook with the greatest room for imagination, letting him play with hundreds of standards before concocting dishes of his own. Shrimp Arnaud, a pungent variation on French rémoulade, is the Count's single most famous creation. The shellfish also turns up in regal Shrimp Bisque and spicy Shrimp Creole.

The Gulf of Mexico and the brackish waters at the mouth of the Mississippi River form one of the country's most important shrimping grounds, with a season from May through December. There is a great variety in color and species—white shrimp, brown shrimp, red and pink shrimp—all graded by the "count." Twenty count, for example, means twenty to the pound. Louisiana shrimp are marketed fresh or frozen in many forms, ranging from whole with the heads on to cooked, peeled, and deveined. As a general rule, it takes about two pounds of raw headless shrimp to get one pound of cooked, peeled, and deveined.

Oysters   These bivalves have been cultivated for at least two thousand years, their name deriving from ancient Greek. Many of the world's coastal regions produce oysters of one kind or another, but the ones grown in Louisiana are hailed as being among the juiciest and briniest anywhere. Most are devoured in their natural state, chilled just a bit to make them more refreshing and lightly brushed past the cocktail sauce. The remaining oysters turn up courtesy of the Creoles in preparations and presentations that seem numberless.

A turn-of-the-century Creole cookbook listed nearly forty oyster recipes, and Arnaud's current menu devotes an entire section to this delicacy. Bienville and Rockefeller are New Orleans' most famous baked oyster dishes, while Oysters Stewed in Cream is a wondrous thick soup. Interestingly, most Louisiana oysters are harvested by fishermen of Yugoslavian descent—their ancestors did much the same off the Adriatic coast of Dalmatia. Oysters are marketed year-round throughout the United States, but they are considered at their peak during the winter months.

Speckled Trout   When the fishermen of Louisiana's bays and bayous took to naming things, sometimes they created sheer poetry. They spotted a white perch and dubbed it a *sac-à-lait,* or bag of milk. Other times they just created confusion. The speckled trout showcased so beautifully in Arnaud's Trout Meunière and Trout Amandine is not really a trout at all but a member of the squeteague-weakfish family. That makes it a relative of croakers, drum, and redfish rather than, for example, the rainbow trout found splashing about in Rocky Mountain streams. All the same, "specks" are beautiful fish to catch—iridescent blue or silver, with black spots along their upper sides—and even more beautiful to eat. One of the mainstays of the Louisiana marketplace, it is offered fresh or frozen, as whole cleaned or boneless fillets. It is available fresh most of the year, with a prime season in May and June, and usually weighs in between one and seven pounds.

Redfish   Touch the black spot near the tail of a redfish and you are touching a legend. According to one story, the redfish was what Christ used to feed the multitude, and the spot was where his thumb touched. Even without the religious significance, this member of the croaker and drum family finds a special place in Creole cuisine. Redfish Courtbouillon is a big, satisfying stew, while Arnaud's Redfish Chambord presents this seafood's sophisticated side—poached, then topped with diced artichokes, mushrooms, and a glaze.

The redfish used for these dishes is found up and down the Atlantic and Gulf coasts, though it is sometimes referred to as channel bass or red drum. Praised for their firm texture and delicious flavor, redfish can run quite large—starting with "rat reds" at ten pounds or less and ranging up to "bull reds" at thirty pounds or more. The best flavor is found among the smaller fish, which are sold fresh or frozen, whole, deboned, or cut into steaks. The larger reds are well-suited for baking, stuffing, boiling, and stewing.

*P*ompano   Mark Twain called the pompano "delicious as the less criminal forms of sin." The locals sometimes call it "sole," placing it squarely in the league of another world-class fish. And most chefs place it far ahead of any sole except Dover. Though pompano range from Massachusetts to Brazil, more are consumed in the United States than anywhere else on the globe. Virtually every famous Creole restaurant has its own special preparation, from the famous Pompano en Papillote to the simple sautéed fillet covered with crabmeat. Movie director Cecil B. DeMille liked the former so much he had it written into the script of *The Pirate's Lady*.

Sometimes called the tastiest fish in America, pompano has firm, rich flesh that carries a subtle reminder of the salty deep. If pompano is unavailable, in recipes calling for it you can substitute a wide variety of similar fish, including red snapper, redfish, mackerel, halibut, and turbot.

Crabmeat   Around New Orleans, the most popular way to enjoy crabs is to boil them with a peppery Creole spice blend, then dump them on a table covered with newspaper, and crack and consume them with icy beer. Yet the meat of the blue crab (sometimes called the Atlantic crab) enlivens some of the finest dishes in the Creole repertoire. Crabmeat Suzanne and Crabmeat Imperial are specialties of Arnaud's, while the flaky white meat also turns up atop trout, pompano, and milk-fed veal.

The crab flourishes in the brackish waters along Louisiana's coastline, especially from April to November. The best blues are four to eight inches from point to point, and they are marketed live whole, cooked whole, or as picked crabmeat in one-pound containers. There are actually three classes of picked crabmeat: lump, the largest section of meat taken from the backfin; special white, all of the body meat; and claw meat, the entire claw shelled with one piece of the pincher left to hold it neatly for dipping.

Turtle   With the possible exception of okra or filé, no ingredient is more important to the Creole soup kitchen than turtle—this despite its traditional prerequisites of a sharp axe and a strong stomach. Today, with the proliferation of commercial turtle farms and frozen or canned turtle meat, there's no reason for aficionados to fret over the words of Creole chef Madame Begue, who begins the first recipe in her 1900 cookbook: "Select a turtle of the desired size, clean it well, and cut in small pieces."

In Louisiana, the favored turtle for making soup is the diamondback terrapin, a saltwater dweller that also relishes the brackish southern marsh. The next best thing is the green sea turtle, when you can find it, or the loggerhead from the Gulf of Mexico, South Atlantic, or Caribbean. There are also Creoles and Cajuns who insist on freshwater turtle—the so-called Cowan sold in some black neighborhood groceries—and most cooks, in a pinch, will accept snappers, leatherbacks, or painted or wood turtles. The soup they make with this meat—thick, creamy, and spiked with sherry— will help you forget any reservations you started with, as well as any pale, thin *soupe de tortue* you tasted elsewhere in the world.

Frog Legs   In the old days, anyone wondering why those spotlights were bobbing through the swamp on a moonless night in spring probably never gave much thought to the glories of the frog. In Louisiana, however, the amphibian called *la grenouille* by the French became so popular it earned a local nickname all its own. With their special talent for poetry, the natives called it *ouaouron,* a strange-looking word that when pronounced, closely resembles the bullfrog's love song.

Today there's no need for the lover of Creole frog dishes to take to the marsh for a night of "gigging." Frogs from commercial farms are available frozen, and usually at reasonable prices. With a flavor similar to quail or pheasant, the legs are the only part that's eaten—usually in some combination of butter, garlic, and parsley. Arnaud's Frog Legs Provençale is a fine example of this preparation. At home, defrosted frog legs should be parboiled for three minutes, then soaked in milk for an hour. Cooking should be handled with care, so the meat's few natural juices do not evaporate. As a main course, allow three or four large (or as many as a dozen small) frog legs per person.

Scallops   With shells so perfect they inspired medieval pilgrims and at least one modern oil company, scallops have long been admired by the Creoles of New Orleans, even though they've never been successful in nearby waters. The city from its beginnings has been too European to ignore Coquilles St. Jacques and a handful of other high-class presentations. In Europe, scallops are sold in their lovely shells, with white muscle and red roe still attached. In the United States, generally only the shelled white muscle is available. Though sometimes sold frozen, scallops should be bought fresh whenever they are available.

Fowl   On the strength of its flavor—and, of course, its availability—chicken was a regular in the old Creole kitchen. It turned up often in gumbos, fricassees, and jambalayas, in well as more formally in Poulet Rochambeau (with both Bordelaise and Béarnaise sauces). The Creoles, however, were avid sportsmen and often supplemented chicken from the market with a wide array of game birds. Fortunately for the modern city-dweller, or the nonhunter anywhere, most of these fowl are now grown commercially and available outside the ebb and flow of their seasons.

Ducks are best fresh-killed, available either from a Chinese market or a friendly farmer; yet the frozen commercially raised five-to-eight-pound ducks usually hailing from Long Island are fine. The important thing is to thaw them beforehand and dry them out thoroughly. Every sliver of meat is great for something, the bones make wonderful soup, and the livers are highly praised.

Quail, those delicate little birds so readily available farm-raised and either fresh or frozen, are another Creole favorite. Broiled or roasted, with the bones they are a bit too messy to serve to company. But boned, stuffed, and baked "au Chambertin" in the style of Arnaud's, they make a truly elegant entrée.

Rock Cornish game hens also enjoy a revered place on Arnaud's menu, thanks to a preparation dreamed up by Germaine Wells. These small birds weigh only about a pound and have been available frozen for quite some time. Increasingly turning up fresh, they are gaining a whole new level of respect from chefs and home cooks alike.

Tripe   It was observed many years ago, supposedly by the late Lucius Beebe, that the enjoyment of tripe was restricted "like certain alluring vices" to the uppermost and lowermost levels of society. Certainly in America, all other levels reject it with a special vehemence. Arnaud's, however, with its strong ties to French tradition, serves tripe in its most famous preparation—*à la Mode de Caen.* The lining of the cow's stomach, tripe varies a great deal in texture, with honeycomb tripe considered the finest for its resemblance to its namesake. Tripe is partially cooked before it is sold, so the proper handling at home is different from one attempt to the next. Tasting alone will determine when it is tender.

Sweetbreads Even among sophisticated diners, many would agree with the *Oxford English Dictionary* that the origin of the name sweetbreads "is not obvious." All the same, there seems to be a growing fondness for these tender thymus glands of calves, whether served as first courses or as main dishes. Occasionally, lamb or beef sweetbreads turn up as well. Because of residual blood that darkens with cooking and clouds broths, the delicacies should be soaked in ice water and blanched or parboiled before being trimmed of the covering membrane and connecting tubes. If the sweetbreads are to be sliced, they should be weighted down until cold. This will impart a firmer, more enjoyable texture.

The Vegetables

Tomatoes Tomatoes are such a glorious part of Creole cooking that there's even a semiofficial variety that pays tribute in its name. You'll hear lots about "Creole tomatoes," even if most people singing their praises have a hard time defining exactly what they are. By way of description, Creole tomatoes are bright red and, like most things dubbed Creole, tend to be found in unusual sizes and shapes. Practitioners of the cuisine are proud of this individuality, as though it offers the ultimate rebuke to perfect but tasteless tomatoes from elsewhere.

If, however, elsewhere is where you get your tomatoes, the

large, vine-ripened ones called "beefsteak" offer the best substitute for the Creoles' lively acid flavor. Avoid the pale hothouse tomatoes if you want your Creole cooking to resemble the real thing; use instead the canned variety, especially the plum-type tomatoes known as *pomodori pelati.*

Onions   In Creole home-cooking, there's a trio of ingredients known as the "Holy Trinity" for, one presumes, its omnipresence. As in most staunchly Catholic towns around the world, this minor bit of sacrilege is tolerated because it is so evocative. And what it evokes best is onions, browning in a pan with green peppers and celery. The Creoles find two types of onions acceptable for chopping and browning, the yellow and the white. The white usually come a bit larger and possess greater pungency, both facets that appeal to the Creole mind.

Scallions and Green Onions   In a Creole city that can't even agree on what Creole means, why be surprised that scallions are beset by confusion as well? No one can figure why they are called shallots locally, even around the colorful stalls of the otherwise-savvy French Market. The real shallot hardly ever turns up in Creole cooking. Scallions, on the other hand, are everywhere. And since green onions are more easily found in the produce bins, they often end up substituting for the scallions referred to as shallots. The green tops are the best part to the Creole way of thinking, giving special texture and flavor to roux, gumbos, and stews. They also make a nifty garnish.

Green Peppers When a Creole cook reaches for his green pepper, you can be sure it isn't jalapeño or some eye-watering variety grown in Thailand. Green sweet peppers, often referred to as "bell peppers" in the South, are an essential ingredient in virtually every Creole classic—and in more than a few Cajun ones as well. In musical parlance, it's as though they, onions, and celery lay down a rhythm for all the other instruments to follow. Members of the *capsicum* genus, green peppers actually turn red or yellow if allowed to fully ripen. You should look for bells that are firm and shapely, rejecting any with discolorations, wrinkles, or soft spots. Before chopping for Creole dishes—or virtually any other kind—remove the stem end, seeds, and white ribs.

Okra This one is a bit of an oddity unless you're from the Deep South, where it's used as a thickener by the Creoles and Cajuns, pickled or fried by just about everyone else. Okra has a long history, including cultivation by the ancient Sumerians and extensive use by the Egyptians (including its pounding to make papyrus). A favorite of African jungle tribes, it reached America with the slaves along with its original name in Tshi—*gombo*. Since the slaves were kept naked during their voyages to bondage, it is said they preserved the gombo seeds just about the only way they could, hiding them in their ears. Today, fresh young okra pods are considered best for adding a unique acidic flavor to Louisiana soups and stews. Frozen okra is thought the next best thing, with canned ranking a little below it.

Mushrooms Despite the nation's current affection for wild mushrooms like *porcini* from Italy or *shiitake* from Japan, these don't do much for Creole dishes. They are certainly not authentic to the recipes, and in general their flavor is too retiring for a robust mix of onions, peppers, celery, and garlic.

So the best way to go is with common fresh mushrooms— don't mention the canned variety in the same breath with any great Creole dish. Or if you happen to know a Cajun who still prefers the swamps to the oil or computer industries, hit him up in the spring for "willow mushrooms," a fungus growing on the trunk of that tree. To Louisiana taste buds, these are every bit as spectacular as the truffles of France and Italy, and you don't even need a pig. All fresh mushrooms should require is a wipe with a damp cloth. If they look dirty, toss them into a colander under running water and dry well before using.

*A*rtichokes   Creoles and Cajuns love these vegetables, which grow nicely in Louisiana's warm, humid climate. The old Creoles contributed Oyster and Artichoke Soup to the pantheon of world cuisine, while the Italian contingent came up with wondrous shrimp-stuffed artichokes. Artichokes can vary greatly in size, from as small as one-inch in diameter up to four inches across the widest part at maturity. Perfect for stuffing *à la Creole,* the larger artichokes should be trimmed by cutting off an inch of their tops and removing the stem and hard leaves around the base.

*M*irlitons   Among the ancient Mayans, this vegetable was known as *chayote.* Among modern Americans, it generally shows up as vegetable pear or custard marrow. Among the Creoles, however, it's the once and future mirliton. Sharing family ties with squash and cucumber, it made its way to Louisiana from points south with the ever-acquisitive Spaniards, immediately finding a place for its mild flavor and receptiveness to stuffing. Delicate seafoods like shrimp and crabmeat work best, especially when slapped awake with Italian herbs and spices.

The Flavorings

Almonds With rave notices going back to Ecclesiastes ("The almond tree shall flourish..."), this is thought by many to be the world's classiest nutmeat. Certainly no Creole would argue after getting up from a dinner built around Trout Amandine. And he might mention that the nuts make an imaginative addition to certain soups and stews. In the kitchen, sliced almonds are strongly preferred to slivered, since the latter are too coarse. Natural or blanched, almonds can be cooked gently in butter—stirred constantly until a deep yellow—before they are used in a savory dish.

G arlic   Once praised as an aphrodisiac, garlic now banks its reputation on doing the next best thing—making just about any dish taste a lot better. With strong contributions from the French, Spanish, and Italians, Creole cuisine was destined to use this bulb with enthusiasm. And it does. Across south Louisiana, there's even a variety called "horse garlic," grown until it's much larger than the imported kind, and sold by farmers from the backs of pickup trucks. Horse garlic is also milder than the imports, so Creole cooks can chop and mince to their hearts' content without overpowering a dish.

Away from the pickup trucks, insist on garlic that is sold fresh, whatever the country on its passport. The powdered or granulated stuff in a bottle just doesn't rate when you're cooking Creole. Full, firm, and heavy heads are best. Before attempting to peel, drop the garlic in boiling water for five seconds or bruise the clove slightly with the flat of a knife blade. Either procedure will loosen the skin, and a touch of salt sprinkled on while chopping keeps garlic from sticking to the knife.

H ot Peppers   Due to the popularity of Cajun food and the global use of a sauce called Tabasco, Louisiana and hot peppers have become virtually synonymous. Although Cajuns do like food with a kick and even Creoles relish a mouth-burn now and again, the cuisine of New Orleans does not rely on hot to the degree of its surrounding countryside. Peppers like the Anaheim chilis, red and green tabascos, serranos, cayennes, jalapeños, and Bahamian reds are more likely to turn up pickled for munching with a cold beer than shoving classic food into a fiery Twilight Zone. If you like peppery food, sauces like Tabasco, Trappey's, Zatarain's, and Crystal add a nice bite to dishes like gumbo or étouffée.

H erbs   These wonders often did double duty in old New Orleans, flavoring the dishes for lunch and dinner while producing health, wealth, romance, or death in the slave religion known as voodoo. Basil in particular found a market with Voodoo Queen Marie Laveau and her many fearful followers, turning up in front yard after front yard to ward off the evil eye. Of course, to do that properly, a male plant with narrow leaves had to grow next to a female plant with broad leaves, a sign for enemies to take their voodoo elsewhere.

All this mysticism aside, Creole cooks have several favorite herbs—among the dried, thyme, basil, bay leaf, filé, oregano, chervil, marjoram, savory, and tarragon; among the fresh, parsley, chives, basil, and thyme. Even if you opt for the dried variety, keep all herbs as fresh as possible, tossing out the leftovers within a few months of their first exposure to air.

S pices   New Orleans picked up many a skill in its long and tangled history, mentionable and otherwise. But none is as essential to the special flavor of its cuisine as the blending of spices. This trial-and-error education must have been all the more difficult with the wild array of taste enhancers pouring in from the Old World and the New. Over the years, cooks settled into an agreement of sorts that certain spices embodied their cuisine, with the main disagreements concerning the proportions. Now, as then, the most frequently used Creole spices are allspice, anise, caraway, cardamom, cinnamon, cumin, ginger, mace, mustard seed, nutmeg, black and white pepper, saffron, and turmeric. These spices are always sold dried, though they can be used either whole or ground. Black pepper does its best work when freshly ground with a mortar and pestle or in a pepper mill.

Filé   Old-fashioned Creole cooks use filé to flavor their gumbos only in the wintertime, though Cajuns tend to dig in
whatever the time of year. Each time a member of either group
turns to the tender green leaves of the sassafras tree, he is nodding
just a bit to the Choctaw Indians. Long before the white man came
to the north shore of Lake Pontchartrain, the Indians were gather-
ing, drying, and grinding sassafras leaves till they became a pungent
powder.

Since it turns stringy if allowed to boil, filé should be added to
gumbo only after it is removed from the fire. In many households,
it is placed on the table for distribution by the diners themselves.
And it should never be used in gumbo with okra, unless you intend
the final product to patch holes in sheetrock.

Filé can be made easily enough once you track down some
sassafras leaves—and made even better if a few bay leaves are
pounded up too. Commercial filé is sold by nearly every grocery
store in south Louisiana, at gourmet shops elsewhere, and by several nationwide mail-order houses.

The Recipes

Appetizers

Mushrooms Jane
—— Serves 6 ——

New Orleanians have always loved the taste combination of fresh mushrooms and lump crabmeat. With the addition of classic touches of fish velouté and glassage, it is worthy of the name Archie Casbarian gave his creation—Jane, for his wife.

36 fresh medium mushrooms (about 1 pound)
Juice of ½ lemon

> *4 cups fresh lump crabmeat*
> *1 1/2 cups finely chopped green onions or scallions*
> *1 1/2 cups Fish Velouté (page 239)*
> *1 cup Glassage (page 240)*

Preheat the oven to 400 degrees.

Remove the stems from the mushrooms and place the caps in a bowl of cold water with the lemon juice, to prevent discoloration. In another bowl, combine the crabmeat, green onions or scallions, and fish velouté. Stuff each mushroom cap with the mixture.

Place 6 mushrooms on each of 6 egg dishes (round platters with decorative ears), or arrange them all on an oval, ovenproof serving dish, and bake for 8 minutes. Remove from oven and ladle about ½ tablespoon of glassage over each stuffed mushroom. Place under the broiler until browned, 20 to 30 seconds. Serve immediately.

Mushrooms Veronique

——————— *Serves 6* ———————

For many years, Trout Veronique has been a favored entrée in fine New Orleans restaurants. As with that main course, the white seedless grape supplies the surprise in this wonderful appetizer. The Boursin cheese gives it taste and substance, while the Parmesan imparts a pleasing brown color after the dish emerges, hot and bubbling, from the oven.

> *36 medium mushrooms (about 1 pound)*
> *36 white seedless grapes (about 1/4 pound)*
> *10 ounces Boursin cheese*
> *1 cup (2 sticks) unsalted butter, melted*
> *2 cups grated Parmesan cheese*
> *Freshly ground black pepper*

Remove the stems from the mushrooms and place a grape in the hollow of each mushroom cap. Using a pastry bag, cover the

grape completely with Boursin. Then carefully dip the entire creation in melted butter and roll it in the grated Parmesan.

Place the mushrooms on a baking sheet or divide them among
individual ovenproof appetizer plates, and refrigerate for 15 minutes.

Preheat the oven to 400 degrees.

Bake the mushrooms for 15 minutes. Top with a bit of black
pepper and serve immediately.

Snails en Casserole
Serves 6

This variation on escargots draws much of its appeal from the ease
with which it can be eaten. There is no need for the usual clamps to hold
the snails while they are drawn from their shells. The puff pastry stands
in for traditional French bread and also assures that the escargots with
their favorite flavorings are piping hot at table.

36 snails, removed from their shells, rinsed, and drained
1⅛ cups Garlic Butter (page 241)
12 ounces fresh or good-quality frozen puff pastry
1 egg, beaten

Preheat the oven to 420 degrees.

Place each snail in a snail pot (available at gourmet and restaurant supply shops) or in any ovenproof dish with a 2-inch diameter.
Cover each snail with garlic butter.

Roll out the puff pastry ⅛ inch thick. Using a 2-inch-diameter
pastry cutter, cut out 36 circles. Cover each snail pot with the puff
pastry, pressing the edges lightly to make sure the puff pastry ad-
heres. Brush the puff pastry with egg. Bake for 8 minutes, or until
the puff pastry turns golden brown. Serve immediately.

Crab Claws Provençale
_____ Serves 6 _____

Arnaud's has a tradition, going all the way back to the Count, of hiring chefs from the south of France, where the rich, demonstrative flavors appeal to visitors from Creole and Cajun Louisiana. At Arnaud's, "Provençale" means a loving application of garlic.

> *¾ cup Garlic Butter (page 241)*
> *1 pound crab claws, with lump of claw meat protruding*
> *6 tablespoons Herbsaint liqueur*
> *Salt and freshly ground black pepper*
> *Pinch of chopped fresh parsley*

Melt the butter in a sauté pan over low heat, then add the crab claws and stir gently until they are hot. Add the Herbsaint and ignite, either by tilting the pan carefully over a gas flame or lighting it with a match. Season to taste with salt and pepper.

Divide the crab claws, shell up, among 6 small round ramekins, 3 inches in diameter. Pour a little of the sauce into each ramekin. Sprinkle with the chopped parsley and serve.

Crabmeat Cocktail
_____ Serves 6 _____

The simple flavors of the sea dominate this cold appetizer, which showcases local crabmeat displayed on a scallop shell.

> *6 Boston lettuce leaves*
> *6 medium scallop shells*
> *4½ cups fresh lump crabmeat (about 2 pounds)*
> *6 pitted California black olives*

6 lemon stars (see Note on page 132)
6 parsley sprigs
³/₄ cup Cocktail Sauce (page 230)

Arrange a lettuce leaf on top of each shell. Top with crabmeat, then decorate with a black olive, lemon star, and parsley sprig. Serve on a doily-lined dinner plate with a small bowl of cocktail sauce on the side.

Artichoke en Surprise
_____ *Serves 6* _____

This cold appetizer adds a dash of pure whimsy to Arnaud's menu. The delightful crabmeat salad is stashed inside the artichoke, waiting to be discovered and devoured.

½ cup flour
½ cup salt
6 fresh medium-sized artichokes
4½ cups Crabmeat Salad (page 206)
6 pitted California black olives
6 parsley sprigs
3 cups shredded iceberg lettuce (about ½ head)
18 tomato slices, halved (about 2 tomatoes)

Fill a large pot with 8 quarts water, add the flour and salt, and bring to a boil over high heat. Add the artichokes and boil for 20 minutes, then remove the pot from the heat and place under cold running water until the artichokes are cold.

Remove the heart from each artichoke, using a teaspoon, and set aside. Clean the interior of the now-exposed bottom, using the spoon to remove any remaining heart, then stuff the artichoke with crabmeat salad. Replace the heart, inverted, and top with a black olive and parsley sprig.

Prepare 6 plates with beds of shredded lettuce. Place the artichokes on top and surround them with tomato slices. Serve immediately.

Crawfish Bourgeois

Serves 6

Named after a man who provided special security services for the restaurant, this is one of those rare dishes at Arnaud's that shouts its Cajun rather than Creole roots. The Tabasco may be adjusted to taste.

½ cup Mayonnaise (page 230)
4 drops Tabasco
2 teaspoons Dijon mustard
1 teaspoon Lea & Perrins sauce
Salt and freshly ground black pepper
2 tablespoons white wine vinegar
1½ pounds Boiled Crawfish Tails (page 233)
6 medium tomatoes
12 pitted California black olives
1 bunch watercress

In a mixing bowl, combine the Mayonnaise, Tabasco, mustard, Lea & Perrins, and salt and pepper to taste. Add the white wine vinegar and blend, then add the crawfish and mix gently. Refrigerate for 10 minutes.

In the meantime, cut the tomatoes in half and scoop out the insides. Fill the tomatoes with the crawfish mixture and top each half with a black olive. Place 2 stuffed tomatoes on each of 6 salad plates. Garnish with watercress and serve.

Marinated Shrimp
_____ *Serves 6* _____

Somewhat predictably, this dish has always been overshadowed by the trademark Shrimp Arnaud, which is a shame considering the distinctive flavor imparted by the marinade. Diners preferring their seafood without sauce often choose this simple yet memorable appetizer.

2½ pounds Boiled Shrimp (page 233)
4 bay leaves
2 cups sliced red onions (about 2 onions)
1½ cups salad oil
¾ cup white wine vinegar
1½ tablespoons salt
2½ tablespoons celery seeds
3 tablespoons capers
⅛ teaspoon Tabasco
1¼ cups shredded iceberg lettuce (about ¼ head)
12 lemon slices
6 cherry tomatoes
6 pitted California black olives

Place a layer of shrimp in a large glass container. Top with 2 of the bay leaves and onion slices. Layer the rest of the shrimp, bay leaves, and onions in this way and set aside. In a bowl, mix the salad oil, vinegar, salt, celery seeds, capers, and Tabasco, and pour the mixture over the shrimp. Cover the container and refrigerate at least 24 hours.

To serve, divide the shredded lettuce among six salad plates. Remove the shrimp from the marinade with a slotted spoon and place 16 to 18 shrimp on each plate. Garnish each serving with 2 slices of lemon, 1 cherry tomato, and 1 black olive.

Oysters on the Half Shell
―――――――――――――――― *Serves 6* ――――――――――――――――

For the purist in any group, here are oysters as Mother Nature made them, glistening in their just-opened shells and ready to be spiked with a pungent dash of Arnaud's Cocktail Sauce.

> *30 cups crushed ice*
> *36 oysters, medium-sized, freshly shucked*
> *¾ cups Cocktail Sauce (page 230)*
> *3 lemons, halved*
> *6 parsley sprigs*

Fill six 9-inch pie pans three-quarters full of crushed ice, then set 6 oysters on each. Place a small cup (about 3 tablespoons) of cocktail sauce at the center of each plate. Garnish with a lemon half and a parsley sprig and serve.

Baked Oysters
―――――――――――――――― *Serves 6* ――――――――――――――――

Dishes involving oysters baked with a complex and flavorful topping form a special part of any great Creole menu. For many New Orleanians, the arrival of a volcano-hot pan of Oysters Bienville or Rockefeller is as essential to the start of a meal as Twelfth Night is to the start of Carnival. And there are just enough variations on these two classic dishes to keep any diner intrigued for a lifetime.

Fortunately for the home cook, preparing New Orleans' greatest oyster dishes is not that difficult—once you have the recipe. For generations, that last was a bit of a problem, since the restaurants that created these formulas refused to go public with them. Now, in this book, Arnaud's shares its methods for the Count's legendary Bienville Topping, along with a surefire version of Rockefeller and several other baked oyster dishes created at the restaurant since Archie Casbarian took over. While

Arnaud's customary presentation has five of the chosen baked oysters per serving, the restaurant also serves a variation for diners hard-pressed to choose. Oysters Arnaud features one oyster each of Bienville, Rockefeller, Suzette, Ohan, and Kathryn. A Creole celebration, to be sure.

Louisiana oysters are most appropriate, of course, but virtually any oyster will do in a pinch. Try for a shell in which the bivalve itself is at least as big as a quarter (a half-dollar is better still) and as plump, juicy, and briny as you can find. As demonstrated below, the oysters are baked on the half shell atop a generous mound of rock salt. This inferior form of salt is not eaten but does a magnificent job of holding the shells steady in the oven and retaining heat at the table.

30 medium oysters, freshly shucked and thoroughly washed
30 medium-sized oyster shells, thoroughly washed
5½ cups topping (recipes below)
12 pounds rock salt
3 lemons, halved
6 parsley sprigs

Preheat the oven to 400 degrees.

Place each oyster on a shell and cover each with approximately 3 tablespoons of the topping of choice. Fill six 9-inch pie pans three-quarters full of rock salt. Place 5 oysters on each pan.

Bake for about 7 minutes, or until the oysters are thoroughly heated. Garnish each serving with a lemon half and parsley sprig. Serve immediately.

Bienville Topping
Yields 5½ cups

¼ cup (½ stick) butter
2 cups small-sized frozen shrimp (90–100 count), chopped
8 cups finely chopped mushrooms
1 cup chopped green onions or scallions

2 teaspoons chopped garlic
1⅓ cups Fish Velouté (page 239)
½ cup milk
¼ cup White Wine Sauce (recipe below)
2 tablespoons brandy
2 bay leaves
2 pinches dried whole thyme
Salt and white pepper
1–2 cups unseasoned bread crumbs

Melt the butter in a pot over high heat, then add the shrimp and cook until pink, about 3 minutes. Add the mushrooms, green onions or scallions, and garlic, stirring for 2 to 3 minutes. Add the fish velouté along with the milk and bring to a boil, then add the white wine sauce, brandy, bay leaves, and thyme.

Return to a boil, reduce heat, and simmer for 5 minutes. Season to taste with salt and white pepper. Add enough bread crumbs to form a paste. Allow to cool completely before spooning on top of the oysters.

White Wine Sauce
Yields 4 cups

While this sauce plays a supporting role in many Arnaud's recipes, it is also delicious when used alone over poached fish.

½ cup chopped shallots
1 cup white wine
4 cups Fish Stock (page 239)
1 Bouquet Garni (page 231)
3 black peppercorns
1 cup heavy cream
2 tablespoons cornstarch
Salt and white pepper

Place the shallots and wine in a saucepan and boil until reduced one third in volume. Add the fish stock and bring to a boil,
then add the bouquet garni and the peppercorns. Reduce the sauce
to about 4 cups, simmering for about 20 minutes.

Add the cream and simmer for 10 minutes. In a small bowl,
mix the cornstarch with 2 tablespoons water, and as the sauce
simmers, add this in small amounts to gradually thicken the sauce
until it coats a spoon. Season to taste with salt and pepper. Strain
through a strainer.

NOTE: White wine sauce can be kept in the refrigerator for up to 1
week, or frozen.

Rockefeller Topping
_____ *Yields 5½ cups* _____

The key to this dish is the parsley-spinach mix, while the Herbsaint
pitches in an identifiable bite.

> 2 tablespoons (¼ stick) butter
> 12 slices raw bacon, chopped
> 4 cups chopped celery
> 1 cup chopped white onions
> 1 cup chopped green peppers
> 2 tablespoons chopped fresh parsley
> 3 tablespoons chopped garlic
> 4 cups chopped, fresh, blanched spinach
> 2 bay leaves
> 2 teaspoons dried basil
> 1 pinch dried whole thyme
> 1 pinch cayenne pepper
> ⅓ cup Herbsaint liqueur
> Salt and freshly ground black pepper

Melt the butter in a pot over high heat, then add the bacon and cook until brown. Add the celery, onions, green peppers, parsley, and garlic, and cook until the onions are translucent. Add the spinach and stir for 7 minutes, then add the herbs and cayenne.

Pour in the Herbsaint and boil for 1 minute, then reduce the heat and simmer for 2 minutes. Season to taste with salt and pepper. Allow to cool completely before spooning on top of the oysters.

Kathryn Topping
Yields 5½ cups

¾ cup (1½ sticks) butter
2¼ cups chopped white onions
3½ cups chopped celery
7½ cups artichoke bottoms or hearts, boiled and chopped
*   (page 242)*
2 bay leaves
Cayenne pepper
¾ cup sherry
3 cups Fish Velouté (page 239)
1 cup unseasoned bread crumbs
Salt and white pepper

Melt the butter in a pot over high heat, add the onions and celery, and cook until transparent. Add the artichokes, followed by the bay leaves and the cayenne to taste, and then by the sherry.

Add the fish velouté and bring to a boil. Reduce the heat and simmer for 4 minutes, then add the bread crumbs and stir until the mixture becomes a paste. Season to taste with salt and white pepper, and remove the bay leaves. Allow to cool completely before spooning on top of the oysters.

Ohan Topping
Yields 5¹/₂ cups

This oyster topping, named after Archie Casbarian's father, is rich with the tastes of the Middle East. The eggplant is a direct reflection of the family's Armenian heritage.

> 1¹/₃ cups olive oil
> 4 pounds eggplant, cut in small cubes
> ³/₄ cup chopped green onions or scallions
> 3 teaspoons dried thyme
> 1 teaspoon dried marjoram
> 1 teaspoon dried oregano
> 3 bay leaves
> 2 cups diced tomatoes, undrained
> 1 teaspoon chopped garlic
> ¹/₃ cup chopped fresh parsley
> Salt and pepper

Heat the olive oil in a pot over high heat. Add the eggplant and sauté for 7 minutes. Add the green onions, thyme, marjoram, oregano, and bay leaves and sauté for 4 minutes. Add the diced tomatoes, bring to a boil, and simmer for 3 minutes.

Add the garlic and chopped parsley, cooking for 5 minutes more. Season to taste with salt and pepper, and remove the bay leaves. Allow to cool completely before spooning on top of the oysters.

Suzette Topping
Yields 5¹/₂ cups

Count Arnaud himself created this baked oyster topping, which derives a zing from the cayenne but not enough to overwhelm the bacon, the vegetables, or the brandy.

⅝ cup (1¼ sticks) butter
6 slices raw bacon, chopped
2⅛ cups chopped celery
3½ cups chopped green onions or scallions
2 tablespoons chopped fresh parsley
2¾ cups chopped red pimentos
2 bay leaves
1 pinch of dried whole thyme
Cayenne pepper
⅜ cup brandy
5⅝ cups Fish Velouté (page 239)
Salt and white pepper

Melt the butter in a pot over high heat. Add the bacon and sauté for 2 minutes. Add all the vegetables (including the pimentos), the herbs, and cayenne to taste, and cook for 3 minutes. Pour in the brandy and fish velouté and boil for 2 minutes, then reduce the heat and simmer for 2 minutes.

Season to taste with salt and white pepper, and remove the bay leaves. Allow to cool completely before spooning on top of the oysters.

Soups

Shrimp Bisque
Serves 6

In New Orleans, shrimp bisque is sure to meet at least three qualifications—rich in flavor, wonderfully creamy, and delightfully warming.

    2 tablespoons (¼ stick) butter
    ½ pound uncooked small shrimp (90–110 count), peeled
    1 tablespoon brandy
    ⅛ cup chopped shallots

¼ cup white wine
¼ cup sliced carrots
¼ cup chopped onions
⅓ cup chopped leeks
½ cup chopped celery
1 tablespoon finely chopped fresh parsley
1 pinch dried basil
1 pinch dried tarragon
1 bay leaf
1 pinch dried oregano
2 pinches dried whole thyme
1 black peppercorn
3 cups Fish Stock (page 239)
⅓ cup tomato purée
Salt and freshly ground black pepper
⅛ cup raw rice
¼ cup heavy cream

Melt the butter in a pot over high heat, then add the shrimp and cook until pink. Flame with the brandy, then add the shallots and mix with the shrimp. Stir in the white wine, followed by all the vegetables, the herbs, and the peppercorn. Stir for 1 minute.

Add the fish stock and 1 quart water and boil for 5 minutes. Add the tomato purée, and season to taste with salt and pepper. Pour in the rice and cook, covered, over medium heat for 10 minutes. Transfer the mixture to a blender or food processor and process for 1 to 2 minutes.

Return the mixture to the pot and bring to a boil. Add the cream, stirring vigorously, and serve immediately.

Gumbo
Serves 6

This great Louisiana favorite, often a meal in itself along the bayous, starts with a heavy brown roux and ends with okra, with flavorful shrimp and crabs added along the way.

3 slices bacon
1/4 cup flour
1/2 cup finely chopped celery
1/2 cup chopped white onions
1/2 cup chopped green onions or scallions
1 teaspoon chopped garlic
1/4 cup chopped green pepper
2 tablespoons chopped fresh parsley
Pinch of dried whole thyme
1 bay leaf
1/2 pound small shrimp (90–110 count)
1/2 pound crabs (claws and body, quartered; see Note below)
1/2 cup diced tomatoes
2 cups Shrimp Stock (page 238)
2 cups sliced okra, sautéed in butter
Salt and freshly ground black pepper
Cayenne pepper

Place the bacon in a pot over high heat and cook until it has rendered its fat. Remove the bacon and use the fat to make a flavorful roux, adding the flour and stirring until the mixture turns brown. The roux should not burn, but the flour must lose its "raw" taste. Reduce the heat and add all the vegetables except the tomatoes and sautéed okra. Add the herbs and cook for 8 minutes.

Add the shrimp and crabs, followed by the diced tomatoes. Pour in the shrimp stock, then bring to a boil. Skim any foam and reduce the heat and simmer for 30 minutes. Add the okra and simmer for 30 minutes more. Skim again and season to taste with salt, black pepper, and cayenne.

NOTE: Quick frozen whole crabs are fine, and frozen crab parts are easiest. To prepare a whole crab (frozen or fresh but *not* alive), peel off the key on the body's bottom and rinse all sand from the inside. Then quarter the body and cut the claws into 2 to 4 pieces each, depending on your preference—smaller perhaps to serve in a cup rather than a large bowl.

Turtle Soup
————————— Serves 6 —————————

The Creoles are fanatics about their soups, demanding that they be prepared exquisitely as well as incessantly. Here is perhaps the single most famous Creole soup, made much easier now by the wide availability of turtle meat.

¼ cup salt
¾ cup fresh or frozen turtle meat
¾ cup ground veal shank meat
6 cups Veal Stock (page 237)
2 cloves garlic, chopped
2 bay leaves
1 pinch of dried whole thyme
3 tablespoons tomato purée
½ cup chopped celery
1 cup chopped green onions or scallions (about 2 bunches)
½ cup chopped white onions (about ½ onion)
1 tablespoon chopped fresh parsley
2 lemons, halved
3 tablespoons sherry
2 eggs, hard-boiled and chopped
Salt and white pepper
2 tablespoons Roux (page 232)

Combine 8 quarts water and half the salt in each of two large pots and bring to a boil over high heat. Place the turtle meat in one, the veal in the other, and simmer both for 45 minutes. Remove both pots from the heat, drain the meat, and chop both meats coarsely in a food processor. Keep warm until needed.

Place the veal stock, garlic, bay leaves, and thyme in a large pot and bring to a boil over high heat. Add the tomato purée, vegetables, parsley, and lemons, and bring back to a boil. Reduce the heat and simmer for 10 minutes.

Add the two kinds of meat and the sherry. Bring to a boil, then reduce the heat and simmer for 5 minutes. Add the eggs, and season to taste with salt and pepper. Thicken by adding small amounts of the roux.

It is customary in New Orleans to serve turtle soup with either a final splash of sherry at the table or with additional sherry available for those who desire it.

Cream of Broccoli Soup
Serves 6

Once you've prepared Arnaud's version of béchamel sauce, the rest of this hearty soup is quick and easy. The flavor and the color of fresh broccoli are preserved against a backdrop of stock and heavy cream.

2 pounds trimmed broccoli
4½ cups Béchamel Sauce (page 225)
1 cup Fish or Chicken Stock (page 239 or 236)
2 cups heavy cream
Salt and white pepper

Cook the broccoli in boiling water for 10 minutes. Drain it, cut off approximately 1 cup of the flowerets, and reserve. Combine the béchamel and broccoli in a pot over high heat and cook for 3 minutes. Add the stock and bring to a boil, then reduce the heat and simmer for 3 minutes. Add the cream.

Transfer the mixture to a blender and purée at high speed for 3 minutes. Return to the pot, and season to taste with salt and pepper. Garnish with the reserved flowerets and serve.

Variation:
Substitute 1¾ pounds fresh asparagus for the broccoli.

Cream of Artichoke Soup
Serves 6

The most difficult part of this preparation is boiling and chopping the artichokes. Once this is done, however, a delicious hot soup can be ready in 10 minutes or less.

> *4½ cups Béchamel Sauce (page 225)*
> *1 cup Fish or Chicken Stock (page 239 or 236)*
> *15 boiled artichoke bottoms (page 242), 12 chopped fine,*
> *3 quartered*
> *2 cups heavy cream*
> *Salt and white pepper*

Heat the béchamel in a pot over medium heat and add the stock. Add the chopped artichokes and boil for 2 minutes, then reduce the heat and simmer for 5 minutes. Add the cream and season to taste with salt and pepper. Garnish with the quartered artichokes and serve immediately.

Onion Soup
Serves 6

Like most restaurants with strong French roots, Arnaud's serves its own variation on this classic soup. Little in this recipe is historic, but the parts all add up to a warm and comforting whole.

> *½ cup goose or duck fat, or butter*
> *2 pounds white onions, thinly sliced*
> *1 cup white wine*
> *2 cups Chicken Stock (page 236)*
> *1 Bouquet Garni (page 231)*
> *White pepper*

Salt
6 slices of French bread, sliced in rounds and toasted
3 cups grated Swiss cheese (about 1 1/2 pounds)

Melt the fat or butter in a large pot over high heat, then add the onions and sauté until brown, stirring often and allowing the pan to sear without burning the onions. This process, which takes about 10 minutes, will give color to the soup.

Deglaze the pan by adding the white wine, and cook for 2 minutes, stirring constantly. Add the chicken stock, bouquet garni, and white pepper to taste. Cook for at least 20 minutes. Remove the bouquet garni, skim the top of the soup, and season to taste with salt.

Divide the soup among 6 crocks. Place 1 slice of bread on top of each and sprinkle with the Swiss cheese. Place under the broiler until the cheese is brown and crusty, 2 to 3 minutes. Serve immediately.

Oysters Stewed in Cream
_____ Serves 6 _____

For those in the know, this is the soup to order at Arnaud's. The cream is carefully prepared and thickened a bit with roux before the poached oysters are added—just moments before serving.

3 1/2 cups water
36 fresh oysters
1 tablespoon butter
1/2 cup chopped celery
1/2 cup chopped green onions or scallions
1/2 cup chopped white onions
1 bay leaf
1 pinch of dried whole thyme
1 pinch of cayenne

> *½ teaspoon chopped garlic*
> *¾ cup heavy cream*
> *2 cups milk*
> *½ cup Roux (page 232)*
> *Salt and white pepper*

Place the water in a pot and bring to a boil over high heat. Add the oysters and poach for 3 minutes, then remove and drain them. Reserve the liquid.

Melt the butter in a pot over high heat. Add the celery, green onions or scallions, and white onions, cooking until they turn translucent. Add the bay leaf, thyme, cayenne, and garlic along with 2½ cups of the oyster water. Bring to a boil.

Pour in the cream, reduce the heat, and simmer for 6 minutes. Add the milk and bring to a gentle boil.

In a separate pan, heat the roux with ½ cup of the oyster water, stirring vigorously until the mixture is soft. Gradually add the roux to the boiling soup to thicken it, stirring until blended after each addition. Add the oysters and season to taste with salt and pepper. Ladle into individual bowls and serve.

Eggs and Omelettes

Eggs Benedict
Serves 6

This classic French preparation, sinfully rich in a sea of hollandaise, is a favorite of the brunch crowd around New Orleans. And for brunch lovers who want to mix the traditional with something a bit more innovative, Arnaud's created Eggs Loftus—one Egg Benedict and one Egg Lafayette (page 123) served in tandem, each topped with its own special sauce.

6 English muffins, halved
12 slices Canadian bacon, cooked to your taste
12 Poached Eggs (page 234)
3 cups Hollandaise Sauce (page 228)
12 slices of pitted California black olives
Paprika to taste
6 parsley sprigs

Toast the English muffin halves and place two on each of 6 dinner plates. Cover each with a slice of Canadian bacon. Top each with a hot poached egg and cover with hot hollandaise.

Top each egg with a slice of olive and sprinkle with paprika. Garnish with a parsley sprig and serve.

Eggs Sardou
Serves 6

This dish, named after Victorien Sardou, the author of *Tosca,* is an interesting twist on Eggs Benedict. And Sardou no doubt would have approved of how the creamed spinach caresses the artichoke bottoms and poached eggs.

4¾ cups Creamed Spinach (page 194)
12 fresh medium-size artichoke bottoms, boiled (page 242)
12 Poached Eggs (page 234)
3 cups Hollandaise Sauce (page 228)
Paprika to taste
6 cherry tomatoes

Spoon the hot creamed spinach into the centers of 6 dinner plates. Center 2 hot artichoke bottoms on top of the spinach. Place a hot poached egg on each artichoke bottom and cover with hot hollandaise. Sprinke with paprika. Garnish each plate with a cherry tomato and serve.

Eggs Hussarde
Serves 6

The custom of brunch—or Creole breakfast—originated as a hearty midmorning meal for butchers and other French Quarter merchants who had not had time for breakfast before reporting for work at dawn. Eggs Hussarde forms a liaison between two great French sauces, making it the perfect brunch selection. To be authentic, begin with a famous New Orleans drink like a gin fizz and round off "breakfast" with a flaming Creole dessert.

> *2¾ cups Bordelaise Sauce (page 226)*
> *12 Holland Rusks (a type of commercial dry biscuit) or*
>   *English muffins*
> *12 slices tomato*
> *12 slices Canadian bacon, cooked to your taste*
> *12 Poached Eggs (page 234)*
> *3 cups Hollandaise Sauce (page 228)*
> *Paprika to taste*
> *6 parsley sprigs*

Spoon the hot Bordelaise sauce into the center of 6 dinner plates. Center 2 Holland Rusks or English muffins on the sauce and top each with a slice of tomato. Place a slice of Canadian bacon on each and top with a hot poached egg.

Cover each serving with hot hollandaise sauce. Sprinkle with paprika, garnish with a parsley sprig, and serve.

Eggs Lafayette
Serves 6

A standby of Arnaud's cuisine is its special Armoricaine sauce—a name that may look strange to even experienced cooks. It has come to be known over the years as Americaine sauce, yet its original name referred to Armorique, an ancient appellation for the Brittany section of France. In this case, it showcases Eggs Lafayette.

3 cups Armoricaine Sauce (page 228)
1¹/₂ cups (24 ounces) Boiled Crawfish Tails (page 233)
12 English muffin halves, toasted
12 Poached Eggs (page 234)
¹/₄ cup chopped fresh parsley

Warm the Armoricaine sauce in a pan over low heat. Add the crawfish and stir gently until the mixture is hot.

Place 2 English muffin halves on each of 6 dinner plates and top each half with a hot poached egg. Cover each egg with the Armoricaine sauce and crawfish mixture. Sprinkle lightly with the chopped parsley and serve.

Eggs Arnaud
————— Serves 6 —————

The name Arnaud on any dish denotes a special pride and care in its preparation. In this case, the restaurant's own Armoricaine sauce makes the creation worthy of the company it keeps at brunch.

3 cups Armoricaine sauce (page 228)
24 ounces fresh lump crabmeat
12 Holland Rusks or English muffins
12 Poached Eggs (page 234)
¹/₄ cup chopped fresh parsley

Warm the Armoricaine sauce in a pan over low heat. Add the crabmeat and stir gently until the mixture is hot.

Place 2 Holland Rusks or English muffins on each of 6 dinner plates and top each Rusk with a hot poached egg. Cover each egg with the Armoricaine sauce and crabmeat mixture. Sprinkle lightly with the chopped parsley and serve.

Omelette New Orleans
Serves 2

With a name like New Orleans, there would almost have to be sea-food somewhere in this omelette. And there is, the delicate flavor and texture of crabmeat bringing distinction, along with Arnaud's Armoricaine sauce. This recipe may be repeated easily for additional servings. Increase all the ingredients accordingly, making the omelettes one at a time in the same pan and setting them aside in a warm place.

> 2 tablespoons (1/4 stick) butter
> 1/2 cup fresh lump crabmeat
> 1/2 cup Armoricaine Sauce (page 228)
> 6 whole eggs
> Salt and freshly ground black pepper
> 2 parsley sprigs

Melt 1 tablespoon of the butter in a pan over low heat, then add the crabmeat and stir. Add the Armoricaine sauce and simmer for approximately 3 minutes.

In the meantime, beat the eggs until they are creamy. Season to taste with salt and pepper. Melt the remaining tablespoon of butter in an omelette pan over medium heat. Pour in the beaten eggs, cook until moist, and fold in half. Remove to a serving dish and cover with the mixture of crabmeat and Armoricaine sauce. Garnish with the parsley sprigs and serve immediately.

Omelette Iberville
Serves 6

This special omelette, named after the French explorer who with his brother Bienville founded the first colonies in Louisiana, reflects the best of what their descendants accomplished in the Creole kitchen.

12 beaten eggs
3 tablespoons virgin olive oil
¾ cup (1½ sticks) butter
½ cup chopped white onions (about ½ onion)
⅓ cup diced tomato (about 1 tomato)
½ cup chopped green pepper (about 1 pepper)
1 teaspoon chopped fresh garlic
1 tablespoon chopped fresh parsley
Salt and freshly ground black pepper
6 parsley sprigs

Heat the olive oil and half the butter in a pan over high heat. Add the onions, tomato, and green pepper. Sauté for 8 minutes. Add the garlic, parsley, and salt and pepper to taste, and sauté for 1 additional minute.

In the meantime, melt the remaining butter in an omelette pan over high heat. Add the beaten eggs and cook without stirring. As soon as the egg mixture begins to harden, about 2 minutes, add the vegetable mixture and stir until blended. Continue to cook until the omelette is firm but retains its moistness, about 2 minutes longer.

Divide among 6 dinner plates. Garnish with the parsley sprigs and serve immediately.

Shellfish

Shrimp Creole

Serves 6

While also a favorite at fine restaurants, Shrimp Creole is most notable as an example of New Orleans home cooking. For all their fancy flourishes, the chefs at Arnaud's remember these roots and serve it local-style on a bed of Louisiana rice.

4 tablespoons virgin olive oil
3 pounds Boiled Shrimp (page 233)

3 cups Creole Sauce (page 227)
Salt and freshly ground black pepper
4½ cups hot, cooked White Rice (page 200)
½ cup chopped fresh parsley

Heat the olive oil in a skillet over high heat. Add the shrimp and stir for a minute, until they are heated through. Add the Creole sauce and bring to a boil. Reduce the heat and simmer for 3 minutes. Season to taste with salt and pepper.

Divide the rice among 6 dinner plates and spoon approximately ½ cup of the sauce over each serving. Sprinkle with the chopped parsley and serve.

Shrimp Clemenceau
—————————————— *Serves 6* ——————————————

Named after the French leader who rose to power during World War I and presided over the Treaty of Versailles, this dish honors the great local shellfish in diplomatic relations with sliced mushrooms, diced potatoes, green peas, and garlic butter.

1½ cups sliced mushrooms
1 lemon wedge
1½ cups diced potatoes
1½ cups (3 sticks) butter, plus 3 tablespoons
1–2 cloves garlic, finely chopped
1¼ cups green peas
2 pounds Boiled Shrimp (page 233)
Salt and freshly ground black pepper

In a sauté pan, cook the mushrooms for about 5 minutes in a small amount of water flavored with a squeeze of lemon and a pinch of salt. In a separate pan, sauté the diced potatoes in the 3 tablespoons butter until they are brown and cooked through.

Melt the remaining 1½ cups butter in a skillet over low heat. Add the peas and heat them, then add the mushrooms and potatoes. After these are hot, add the shrimp and stir them gently until heated. Season to taste with salt and pepper, and serve.

Shrimp Derval
Serves 6

An intriguing shrimp dish, this goes to the heart of traditional America by mixing the flavors of bourbon and corn. It took many experiments to find just the right balance, but the finished product proved worth the trouble. The dish is named after the Arnaud's sous-chef who created it.

> *4 tablespoons (½ stick) butter*
> *4 pounds raw shrimp (40–50 count), headless, peeled, and*
>   *deveined*
> *½ cup finely chopped shallots*
> *1½ cups fine bourbon whiskey (preferably Daviess County)*
> *12 ounces frozen kernel corn, thawed*
> *4½ cups heavy cream*
> *Salt and cayenne pepper*

Melt the butter in a pan over high heat, then add the shrimp and cook until they are pink, about 3 minutes. Add shallots and cook until they are translucent. Add the bourbon and ignite it, either by tipping the pan over a gas flame or lighting it carefully with a match. Allow the flames to burn out.

Add the corn and stir. Remove the shrimp with a slotted spoon and set aside. Add the cream and reduce the sauce until it coats a spoon. Return the shrimp to the pan and bring the sauce to a boil. Season to taste with salt and cayenne. Serve immediately.

Shrimp au Gratin

———————————— *Serves 6* ————————————

Seafood and cheese have proven a winning combination over the years. This entrée blends Mornay sauce with both Swiss and Parmesan to envelop fresh shrimp in a wonderful way.

> *1 tablespoon butter*
> *3 teaspoons chopped shallots*
> *2 pounds raw shrimp, 26–30 count, headless, peeled, and*
> *deveined*
> *6 tablespoons white wine*
> *Salt and freshly ground black pepper*
> *2¼ cups Mornay Sauce (recipe below)*
> *3 teaspoons grated Swiss cheese*
> *3 teaspoons grated Parmesan cheese*

Melt the butter in a pan over high heat, then add the shallots and sauté until translucent. Add the shrimp and cook until they turn pink, about 3 minutes. Pour in the white wine and cook for 2 minutes, then season to taste with salt and pepper. Add the Mornay sauce and Swiss cheese. Boil for 1 minute.

Pour the mixture into each of 6 egg dishes or oval-shaped ovenproof serving dishes. Sprinkle each serving with ½ teaspoon of Parmesan cheese and place under the broiler until golden brown, about 20 seconds. Set the hot dishes on doily-covered plates and serve.

Mornay Sauce

———————————— *Yields 1 quart* ————————————

> *1 quart Béchamel Sauce (page 225)*
> *1 cup grated Swiss cheese*
> *1 pinch nutmeg*

Place the béchamel in a pot and bring to a boil over high heat. Reduce the heat and simmer for 2 minutes, then remove from the heat. Add the cheese slowly, stirring with a wire whisk until blended. Add the nutmeg while continuing to stir.

NOTE: Mornay sauce can be kept for up to two days in the refrigerator.

Stuffed Shrimp Carl
Serves 6

Here is a marvelous variation on the fried shrimp so popular in New Orleans—one that's perfect for lunch or brunch. A hearty stuffing of crabmeat, bread crumbs, and seasonings is the key.

18 raw shrimp (26–30 count), headless
1½ pounds fresh lump crabmeat
½ cup chopped green onions or scallions (about 1 bunch)
3 tablespoons chopped fresh parsley
10 eggs
1 pinch of cayenne pepper
Salt and freshly ground black pepper
4 cups unseasoned bread crumbs
1 cup flour
4 quarts vegetable oil
6 large Boston lettuce leaves
6 lemon stars (see Note below)
¼ cup Tartare Sauce (recipe below)

Preheat the oven to 350 degrees.

Peel the shrimp except for the tail and butterfly them, slicing them open along the back and removing the small black vein.

In a mixing bowl, combine the crabmeat, green onions, parsley, 4 of the eggs, the cayenne and salt and pepper to taste. Mix well, then slowly add 1½ cups of the bread crumbs until the mixture is thick but still moist. Wrap the stuffing snugly around the butterflied shrimp, leaving the tail exposed.

In a fryer or large pot, heat the vegetable oil to 350 degrees. Meanwhile, in 3 separate bowls, place the flour, the remaining 2½ cups bread crumbs, and the remaining 6 eggs, which have been beaten. Dip the stuffed shrimp in the flour, then in the eggs, and then in the bread crumbs.

When the oil reaches 350 degrees, place the shrimp in it a few at a time and cook until golden brown, approximately 7 minutes. Remove the shrimp with a slotted spoon. Drain on paper towels and transfer to a baking sheet. After all the shrimp have been fried, transfer them to the oven and bake for an additional 4 minutes.

Place a lettuce leaf on each of 6 dinner plates. Top each with 3 shrimp, garnish with a lemon star, and serve with tartare sauce.

NOTE: To prepare a lemon star as an elegant alternative to a lemon wedge, hold a lemon upright and slice a bit off the top and bottom to create flat surfaces. Then insert the knife at an angle halfway through, and while turning the lemon, make angled cuts that resemble the points of a crown. When the circle is completed, the "star" will appear as the lemon halves separate. The flat surface allows these halves to sit steadily on plates.

Tartare Sauce
Yields about 2 cups

> 1¼ *cups homemade or good-quality Mayonnaise (page 230)*
> 1 *tablespoon Creole mustard*
> ¼ *tablespoon Dijon mustard*
> ¼ *cup chopped fresh parsley*
> ¼ *cup chopped green onions or scallions*
> 2 *tablespoons chopped kosher dill pickles*

1½ teaspoons lemon juice
1–2 drops Tabasco
1 hard-boiled egg, chopped
Salt and white pepper

Using a blender at low speed, blend the mayonnaise and two types of mustard for 2 minutes. Add the parsley, green onions or scallions and pickles and blend for 1 minute. Add the lemon juice and Tabasco, blending for 2 minutes more. Add the chopped egg and blend for 30 seconds. Season to taste with salt and white pepper.

NOTE: Tartare sauce can be kept, covered, in the refrigerator for up to 2 weeks.

Crabmeat Suzanne
———————————— *Serves 6* ————————————

This entrée is a perfect symbol for Arnaud's, an establishment that reveres the past yet welcomes the future. Added to the menu under Archie Casbarian, Crabmeat Suzanne keeps its bounty piping hot in a delightfully crafted puff pastry crab, complete with golden brown claws.

1 cup finely chopped fresh mushrooms (about ½ pound)
¾ cup finely chopped green onions or scallions
3 eggs, beaten
¼ cup heavy cream
Salt and white pepper
Cayenne pepper
13 ounces fresh lump crabmeat
1 cup unseasoned bread crumbs
4 pounds fresh puff pastry or 2 sheets good-quality frozen
¾ cup White Wine Sauce (page 108)
6 cherry tomatoes
6 parsley sprigs

Preheat the oven to 375 degrees.

In a large bowl, combine the mushrooms; the green onions or scallions; ⅓ of the beaten eggs; the cream; and the salt, white pepper, and cayenne to taste. Mix well. Add the crabmeat and mix gently. Add the bread crumbs and mix.

Though the next step can be handled free-hand, it is best to use a crab-shaped pastry cutter about 7 by 4 inches, available at gourmet shops and restaurant supply houses. Roll out the puff pastry to ⅛ inch in thickness, and cut into 12 crab shapes.

Spoon ⅙ of the crabmeat mixture into the center of the 6 shells, leaving a border of ½ inch on all sides. Then brush beaten egg onto exposed puff pastry. Place the remaining crab-shaped shells on top, covering the mixture. Seal by pinching the edges with your fingers. Brush the entire pastry surface with beaten egg.

Carefully place the stuffed pastries on a sheet pan and bake for 20 minutes, or until golden brown.

In the meantime, heat the white wine sauce gently over low heat. When the pastries are ready, ladle about 2 tablespoons of hot white wine sauce onto each of 6 dinner plates. Center a crab pastry on the sauce, then garnish with a cherry tomato and a parsley sprig. Serve immediately.

Crabmeat Monaco
Serves 6

From the Count's day to the present, Arnaud's chefs have honored classical technique while adding touches of their own, as in this dish. This traditional preparation proves a happy home for New Orleans' fresh crabmeat.

½ cup Garlic Butter (page 241)
1½ cups finely sliced mushrooms (about ¾ pound)
½ cup chopped green onions or scallions

½ cup chopped shallots
⅛ cup chopped garlic
½ cup diced tomato
¼ cup tomato purée
3 whole bay leaves
2 pinches whole thyme
2½ pounds fresh lump crabmeat
¾ cup Glassage (page 240)
6 lemon stars (see Note on page 132)
6 parsley sprigs

Melt the garlic butter in a pan over high heat, then add the mushrooms, green onions or scallions, shallots, and garlic, and sauté for 3 minutes. Add the diced tomato, tomato purée, bay leaves, and thyme, and bring the mixture to a boil for 3 minutes. Lower the heat and simmer for 5 minutes. Add the crabmeat and bring back to a boil for 4 minutes.

Divide the mixture evenly into 6 oval ramekins. Cover each with approximately 2 tablespoons glassage. Brown quickly under the broiler for about 10 seconds. Serve on a doily-lined dinner plate, garnished with a lemon star and a parsley sprig.

Crabmeat Imperial
Serves 6

Here is a dish found regularly outside New Orleans but one that gets special attention and affection here. The red and green peppers contribute color, while the Dijon mustard tosses in a pleasurable zing.

6 tablespoons (¾ stick) butter
⅜ cup finely chopped white onions
¼ cup finely chopped pimento
⅜ cup finely chopped green peppers
¾ cup white wine

½ cup Dijon mustard
3 cups heavy cream
24 ounces fresh lump crabmeat
Salt and freshly ground black pepper
Cayenne pepper
¾ cup Glassage (page 240)

Melt the butter in a sauté pan over low heat, then add the onions, pimento, and green peppers, cooking until translucent, about 4 minutes. Add the wine and reduce by half over high heat, about 5 minutes.

Add the Dijon mustard and stir. Add the cream and reduce the sauce until it coats a spoon, about 3 minutes. Add the crabmeat and stir gently until hot, another 6 to 7 minutes. Season to taste with salt, pepper, and cayenne. Divide equally among 6 ovenproof dishes. Top with glassage and brown under the broiler, about 10 seconds. Serve.

Scallops Hoffman
_____ Serves 6 _____

Named after the attorney who worked with Archie Casbarian from the day he took over Arnaud's, this dish has a bit of a generational saga. It started life as Mussels Hoffman, a nifty nickname for a lawyer but apparently no great love of Arnaud's clientele. The preparation remains, now applied to more popular scallops instead. And those in the know now say hello to "Scallops" when they spot him in the restaurant.

14½ ounces fresh or good-quality frozen puff pastry
1 egg, beaten
¼ cup finely chopped shallots
2 cups Fish Stock (page 239)
2¾ pounds medium bay scallops, removed from shell and
   with coral removed

2 tablespoons (¹/₄ stick) butter
1 cup finely sliced fresh mushrooms (about ¹/₂ pound)
1 cup finely sliced leeks (about 1 medium leek)
1¹/₃ cups finely sliced carrots (about 2 medium carrots)
4¹/₂ cups White Wine Sauce (page 108)
Salt and freshly ground black pepper
Pinch of chopped fresh parsley

Preheat the oven to 370 degrees.

Roll out the puff pastry to ¹/₈ inch thick and cut out twelve 4-inch squares. From half these squares, cut out a 2-inch square and discard, leaving the 1-inch border. Set one of these forms carefully atop each of the unaltered squares.

Brush each pastry square with beaten egg. Place them all on a baking pan and bake in the oven for about 15 minutes, or until the pastry rises and browns.

Meanwhile, place the shallots and fish stock in a saucepan and bring to a boil over high heat. Add the scallops and return to a boil, then reduce the heat and simmer for 7 minutes. Remove from the heat and strain.

Melt the butter in a sauté pan over high heat, then add the mushrooms, leeks, and carrots, cooking until the leeks begin to look translucent. Add the drained scallops and white wine sauce and bring to a boil. Reduce the heat and simmer for 3 minutes.

Season to taste with salt and pepper, and spoon the mixture into each of the puff pastry squares. Sprinkle with the chopped parsley and serve immediately.

Scallops Scott
Serves 6

This is an exceedingly unusual dish for Arnaud's, created by a sous-chef no doubt under the spell of the East. It is a perfect light lunch or dinner, with the apples providing a crunch along with a sweet counterpoint to the curry.

⅓ cup (⅔ stick) butter
2 pounds medium bay scallops, removed from shell and with
*   coral removed*
4 tablespoons chopped shallots
3 tablespoons brandy
2 cups White Wine Sauce (page 108)
2 tablespoons curry powder
1½ unpeeled Washington or other red apples, thinly sliced
Salt and freshly ground black pepper
6 cherry tomatoes
6 parsley sprigs

Melt the butter in a pan over high heat, add the scallops, and sauté for 3 minutes. Drain away the liquid and add the shallots, sautéeing for 1 minute more. Pour in the brandy and flame, either by tilting the pan over a gas flame or lighting carefully with a long match.

When the flames have burned out, add the white wine sauce along with the curry powder and boil for 2 minutes. Add the apples, then season to taste with salt and pepper. Divide among 6 warmed dinner plates, garnish each with a cherry tomato and a parsley sprig, and serve immediately.

Coquilles St. Jacques Provençale
_____ Serves 6 _____

Here is another fine example of Arnaud's long-running love affair with the south of France, employing sweet-tasting bay scallops in their single most famous presentation. The reference to St. Jacques (St. James in English, Santiago in Spanish) comes from medieval pilgrims who walked across southern France to Santiago de Compostela in Spain. These

men and women chose the scallop, or cockleshell, as their emblem, carrying it atop a walking staff as a symbol of their faith.

> 42 ounces medium bay scallops, removed from shell and with
>   coral removed
> Salt and white pepper
> 1/2 cup flour
> 6 tablespoons (3/4 stick) butter
> 1/4 cup Herbsaint liqueur
> 2 cups finely chopped green onions or scallions
> 2/3 cup diced fresh tomatoes
> 1/4 cup finely chopped garlic
> 1 cup Glassage (page 240)

Season the scallops to taste with salt and pepper, then sprinkle
lightly with the flour. Melt the butter in a sauté pan over high heat,
add the scallops, and sear. Carefully pour off the remaining butter,
add the Herbsaint, and flame, either by tilting the pan slightly over
a gas flame or lighting with a long match.

When the flames have burned out, add the green onions or
scallions, tomatoes, and garlic and stir for approximately 3 minutes.
Divide the mixture evenly into 6 small casserole dishes (about 8
scallops to a portion). Top each serving with 2 generous tablespoons of glassage, brown under the broiler for about 10 seconds,
and serve immediately.

Crawfish Wellington
Serves 6

Though at first it seems an odd tip of the hat to familiar Beef Wellington, this dish is a wonderful variation spotlighting Louisiana's most versa-
tile shellfish. A filling of crawfish tails, mushrooms, and scallop mousse is
sealed in puff pastry and served in a pool of White Butter Sauce.

1 cup (½ pound) Boiled Crawfish Tails, cut in half (page
   233)
2 cups Scallop Mousse (recipe below)
1 tablespoon brandy
4 cups sliced fresh mushrooms, about 1½ pounds
Salt and freshly ground black pepper
4 pounds fresh or good-quality frozen puff pastry
2 eggs, beaten
¾ cup White Butter Sauce (recipe below)
6 parsley sprigs

Preheat the oven to 350 degrees.

Mix the crawfish, scallop mousse, and brandy in a bowl, and
set aside. Then, in a pan over high heat, sauté the mushrooms until
the moisture in them has evaporated. Season to taste with salt and
pepper.

Roll out the puff pastry to ⅛ inch thick and cut 6 rectangles 7
by 5 inches. Center 1 teaspoon of the sautéed mushrooms on each
rectangle, then top with about ½ cup of the crawfish mixture. Cover
with another teaspoon of the mushrooms.

Brush all the exposed puff pastry with beaten egg, fold over
the edges, and seal by pinching lightly. Decorate with any excess
pastry cut into interesting shapes. Brush all the surfaces with egg
and place the pastries on a sheet pan.

Bake in the oven for 22 minutes, until the pastry turns golden
brown. When ready to serve, ladle 2 tablespoons of white butter
sauce on each of 6 dinner plates. Center the Wellington shells on
the sauce, garnish with the parsley sprigs, and serve immediately.

Scallop Mousse
_____ Yields 2 cups _____

1½ pounds medium bay scallops, removed from shell (with
   coral removed), drained

4 eggs
1 cup heavy cream
Salt and white pepper
4 tablespoons finely chopped carrots
4 tablespoons finely chopped leeks
4 tablespoons chopped fresh parsley
1 pinch of cayenne pepper
½ cup bread crumbs, approximately

Place the scallops in a blender and blend until light and smooth. Add the eggs and heavy cream, then season to taste with salt and white pepper. Blend for 2 minutes more at high speed.

While continuing to blend, add the carrots, leeks, parsley, and cayenne. Blend until a smooth mousse is achieved, thickening as needed with the breadcrumbs.

White Butter Sauce
Yields 2 cups

⅛ cup chopped shallots
¼ teaspoon coarse white pepper
1½ cups dry white wine
¼ cup heavy cream
½ cup (1 stick) butter
Salt

Combine the shallots, white pepper, and wine in a pot. Bring to a boil over high heat, then reduce the heat and simmer until the liquid has almost evaporated. Add the cream and reduce to one-third volume.

Remove from the heat and add the butter, small amounts at a time, whipping with a whisk until the butter is completely mixed with the cream. (The sauce will separate if this is done over heat.) Season to taste with salt.

NOTE: White butter sauce cannot be stored, but any leftovers are good over a sophisticated salad.

Crawfish O'Connor
_____ Serves 6 _____

Named after a friend of Archie Casbarian's, in this dish the crawfish tails are flamed in brandy before honoring them with one of the restaurant's favorite sauces, Armoricaine. A bright red boiled crawfish in the shell makes a wonderful garnish.

> *¾ cup (1½ sticks) butter*
> *1⅛ cups finely chopped shallots*
> *1 cup (½ pound) Boiled Crawfish Tails (page 233)*
> *6 tablespoons brandy*
> *6 tablespoons heavy cream*
> *2¼ cups Armoricaine Sauce (page 228)*
> *Salt and freshly ground black pepper*
> *Cayenne pepper*
> *Pinch of chopped fresh parsley*

Melt the butter in a sauté pan over high heat, add the shallots, and cook until translucent, about 4 minutes. Add the crawfish tails, and sauté 6 to 7 minutes, stirring often. Add the brandy and flame, either by tilting the pan over a gas flame or igniting the liquid with a long match.

Add the whipping cream and bring to a boil, then reduce the heat and simmer for 2 minutes. Add the Armoricaine sauce and bring to a boil. Reduce the heat and simmer for 3 minutes. Season to taste with salt, pepper, and cayenne. Sprinkle the chopped parsley on top and serve immediately.

Fish

Trout Meunière

Serves 6

Count Arnaud gave this traditional dish a new twist by deep-frying the trout—and fleshing out the traditional French meunière sauce of butter, parsley, and lemon.

> *6 fresh speckled trout fillets, each approximately 8 ounces*
> *1½ cups milk*
> *1½ cups flour*

> 2¹/₂ *cups vegetable oil*
> 1¹/₂ *cups Meunière Sauce (recipe below)*
> 6 *lemon stars (see Note on page 132)*
> 6 *parsley sprigs*

Heat the oil to 350 degrees in a skillet over high heat.

Dip the fillets in milk, then dredge in the flour on both sides and shake off any excess. Place the fillets in the heated oil and fry for approximately 8 minutes, until golden brown. Remove and drain.

Ladle ¼ cup of meunière sauce on each of 6 dinner plates and place the fillets on the sauce. Garnish each with a lemon star and a parsley sprig and serve immediately.

Meunière Sauce
_____ *Yields 2 cups* _____

> 2 *tablespoons (¹/₄ stick) butter*
> ¹/₂ *stalk celery, chopped*
> ¹/₄ *cup chopped fresh parsley*
> ¹/₂ *white onion, halved*
> ¹/₄ *cup chopped green pepper*
> ¹/₂ *lemon, halved*
> ¹/₄ *teaspoon black peppercorns*
> 1 *Bouquet Garni (page 231)*
> 1 *clove*
> 1 *clove garlic, halved*
> 1¹/₂ *cups Veal Stock (page 237)*
> 1 *tablespoon lemon juice*
> 3 *tablespoons Roux (page 232)*
> *Salt and freshly ground black pepper*

Melt the butter in a saucepan over high heat. Add all the vegetables, the lemon, and the seasonings (except the salt and ground pepper), and sauté until brown. Add the veal stock and the lemon juice, then bring to a boil for 2 minutes, reduce the heat, and simmer for 10 minutes.

Add the roux a tablespoon at a time until the sauce coats a spoon. Season to taste with salt and pepper. Strain through a strainer and serve.

NOTE: Meunière sauce can be kept in the refrigerator for up to 1 week.

Trout Amandine
———————————— Serves 6 ————————————

New Orleans has loved this buttery combination of trout and sliced almonds for generations, and Count Arnaud lured many a diner from other French Quarter restaurants with his version.

> *6 fresh speckled trout fillets, each approximately 8 ounces*
> *1½ cups flour*
> *1 cup (2 sticks) butter*
> *Juice of ½ lemon*
> *1½ cups almonds, sliced and toasted (see Note below)*
> *6 lemon stars (see Note on page 132)*
> *6 parsley sprigs*

Dredge each fillet in the flour on both sides, then shake off any excess. Melt about ⅓ cup of the butter in a pan over high heat. Add the fillets and sauté approximately 5 minutes on each side.

In a separate pan, melt the remaining butter over low heat. Add the juice from the lemon half and stir. Place each of the fillets in a dinner plate, cover with the almonds, and top with the lemon and butter sauce. Garnish with a lemon star and parsley sprig. Serve immediately.

NOTE: To toast almonds, place them on a roasting pan and set on the bottom rack of a broiler. They burn very fast, so be careful. Remove as soon as they turn golden, about 1 minute.

Trout Leslie
_____ *Serves 6* _____

Carrot and cucumber balls, and chopped hazelnuts make this an unusual dish for a classic Creole restaurant. Yet its presentation and taste have earned it many friends among Arnaud's regulars.

>*2 cups Courtbouillon (page 234)*
>*6 fresh speckled trout fillets, each approximately 6 ounces*
>*1 cup White Wine Sauce (page 108)*
>*1/2 cup heavy cream*
>*1/8 cup carrot balls (use melon baller #10)*
>*1/8 cup cucumber balls (use melon baller #10)*
>*3/4 cups chopped hazelnuts*
>*Salt and freshly ground black pepper*
>*6 lemon stars (see Note on page 132)*
>*6 parsley sprigs*

Bring the courtbouillon to a boil in a pot over high heat, then add the trout and poach for 6 to 7 minutes.

In the meantime, bring the white wine sauce to a boil in a pan over high heat. Add the cream and return to a boil, then reduce the heat and simmer for 3 minutes. Add the carrots, cucumbers, and hazelnuts and simmer for 1 minute. Season to taste with salt and pepper.

Place a trout fillet on each of 6 dinner plates and cover with the sauce. Garnish with a lemon star and parsley sprig. Serve immediately.

Pompano en Croûte
Serves 6

Though classic French in origin, this dish was quite an innovation when it turned up in New Orleans shortly after Archie Casbarian took over Arnaud's. It was the first of the *en croûte* specialties he added to the menu, and it remains far and away the most popular.

> *1½ pounds medium scallops, removed from shells and with coral removed*
> *¼ cup finely chopped carrots*
> *½ cup finely chopped celery*
> *1 tablespoon finely chopped shallots*
> *2 tablespoons heavy cream*
> *3 eggs, beaten*
> *1 teaspoon salt*
> *¼ teaspoon white pepper*
> *1 pinch of cayenne pepper*
> *1 pinch of nutmeg*
> *½ cup unflavored bread crumbs*
> *1⅓ pounds fresh or good-quality frozen puff pastry*
> *12 thinly sliced fresh pompano fillets, each approximately 2 ounces*
> *1½ cups Green Peppercorn Sauce (recipe below)*
> *6 parsley sprigs*

Preheat the oven to 350 degrees.

Chop the scallops in a food processor or blender, pulsing on and off carefully until they form a mousse. Add the carrots, celery, and shallots and blend. Transfer to a mixing bowl and add the cream, one-third of the beaten eggs, the salt, white pepper, and the cayenne and nutmeg according to taste. Mix gently with a rubber spatula, then add the bread crumbs and mix thoroughly.

Roll out the puff pastry to ⅛-inch thicknesss on a lightly floured board. Using a pastry cutter in the form of a fish (8½-by-5½ inches is perfect), cut twelve ⅛-inch-thick shells of puff pastry. Center one pompano fillet on each of 6 shells, top with one-sixth of the scallop-vegetable mixture, and cover with another fillet.

Brush all the exposed puff pastry with beaten egg. Cover with a second pastry shell and seal by crimping the edges with the fingers. Using small pieces of remaining puff pastry, form eyes, gills, scales, and a tail to decorate the fish-shaped shells. Brush with beaten egg.

Place on a sheet pan and bake for 20 minutes, until the pastry turns golden brown. When the pastry is ready, spoon about ¼ cup of green peppercorn sauce onto each of 6 dinner plates. Center the shell on the sauce, garnish with a parsley sprig, and serve immediately.

Green Peppercorn Sauce
Yields 2 cups

2 tablespoons (¼ stick) butter
⅛ cup chopped shallots
½ cup white wine
2 cups Fish Stock (page 239)
1 clove garlic, chopped
1 Bouquet Garni (page 231)
1 tablespoon green peppercorns
1½ tablespoons cornstarch
Salt
½ cup chopped green onions or scallions
½ cup heavy cream

Melt the butter in a large saucepan over high heat, then add shallots and cook until translucent. Add the white wine, fish stock, garlic, and bouquet garni. Increase the heat and reduce the liquid to one-third its volume, approximately 8 minutes.

Add the green peppercorns and bring to a boil, then reduce the heat and simmer for 10 minutes. In a small bowl, dissolve the cornstarch in an equal amount of water and add in small amounts to gradually thicken the sauce until it coats a spoon.

Season to taste with salt, then add the green onions or scallions, followed by the cream. Bring to a boil for 5 minutes and remove the bouquet garni.

NOTE: Green peppercorn sauce can be kept in the refrigerator for several days.

Pompano Pontchartrain
Serves 6

In a minor rebellion against the sauces that enliven their cuisine, many New Orleanians have developed a special affection for this marriage of two favorite seafoods, simply graced with a touch of tangy lemon butter.

1½ cups flour
Salt and white pepper
6 fresh pompano fillets, each approximately 8 ounces
1¼ cups (2½ sticks) butter
3 cups Sautéed Crabmeat (page 232)
¾ cup Lemon Butter (page 241)
6 lemon stars (see Note on page 132)
6 parsley sprigs

Season the flour to taste with salt and white pepper, then dredge the fillets and shake off any excess. Melt the butter in a sauté pan over high heat, then add the fillets and cook for 4 minutes on each side.

Place the fillets on dinner plates and cover each with about ½ cup of crabmeat. Top each with approximately 2 tablespoons lemon butter. Garnish each with a lemon star and a parsley sprig. Serve immediately.

Pompano Bayaldi en Papillote
Serves 6

This dish is, in a sense, nouvelle cuisine's answer to traditional Pompano en Papillote. Its tastes and textures remain more distinct in this presentation, thanks to the relatively brief cooking time. And by the way, always slice open the bag in front of each guest—the release of aroma is dramatic.

Parchment or waxed paper
2 tablespoons Garlic Butter (page 241)
6 fresh pompano fillets, each approximately 7 ounces
Salt and freshly ground black pepper
4 medium tomatoes, sliced
2 pounds zucchini, sliced
2 pinches dried whole thyme
2 tablespoons virgin olive oil

Preheat the oven to 350 degrees.

Cut the parchment or waxed paper in 6 sheets about 15 inches square. Fold each sheet of paper in two and, using scissors, round off the unfolded edges. Unfold each sheet on a flat surface.

Place a small amount of garlic butter on the side of each square sheet, dividing the butter about equally. Top the butter with a fillet of pompano, then season to taste with salt and pepper.

Top the fillet with alternating slices of tomato and zucchini, using 3 of each on each fillet. Season again to taste, add the thyme, and sprinkle lightly with the olive oil.

Fold the paper over as before and pinch the edges to seal, forming a bag filled with pompano and vegetables. Place the bags in a roasting pan into which you have poured ⅛ inch of water. The water will keep the bags from burning and also provide steam to inflate them.

Set the roasting pans in the preheated oven for 7 minutes, then transfer each bag to a warmed dinner plate and serve immediately. With a sharp knife, slice open each bag in front of a diner and fold back the paper to let the aroma escape upward.

Pompano Loeb
———————— Serves 6 ————————

Belgian endives join the more familiar shallots and garlic to flavor this wonderful pompano dish. The sauce of heavy cream tinged with tomato purée and lemon juice blends beautifully with the pompano's tender white flesh.

> 1/2 cup (1 stick) butter
> 6 fresh pompano fillets, each approximately 7 ounces
> 1/2 cup flour
> 1/2 cup chopped shallots
> 2 whole Belgian endives, thinly sliced across
> 1/4 teaspoon chopped garlic
> 1 cup heavy cream
> 2 tablespoons tomato purée
> 2 tablespoons lemon juice
> Salt and white pepper
> 6 lemon stars (see Note on page 132)
> 6 parsley sprigs

Melt 6 tablespoons of the butter in a pan over high heat. Dip the pompano fillets in the flour and shake off any excess, then place them in the pan and cook for 3 minutes on each side.

In the meantime, melt the remaining 2 tablespoons butter in a separate pan over high heat, then add the shallots, endive slices, and garlic and cook for 4 minutes. Add the cream and bring to a boil. Lower the heat, add the tomato purée, and simmer for 2 minutes. Add the lemon juice and season to taste with salt and white pepper.

Place the pompano fillets on dinner plates and cover with the sauce. Garnish each portion with a lemon star and parsley sprig, then serve immediately.

Redfish Arnaud

———————————— *Serves 6* ————————————

A perfect response to both nouvelle and American cuisines, this dish combines two perennial winners—redfish and lump crabmeat—with the simple adornments of butter and lemon.

> *12 eggs*
> *1 pinch each of salt and white pepper*
> *6 fresh redfish fillets, each approximately 8 ounces*
> *1½ cups flour*
> *1⅝ cups (3¼ sticks) butter*
> *2 tablespoons lemon juice*
> *3 cups Sautéed Crabmeat (page 232)*
> *6 lemon stars (see Note on page 132)*
> *6 parsley sprigs*

Beat the eggs until creamy and season with the salt and pepper, then dredge each fillet in the flour, shake off any excess, and dip in the egg mixture.

Melt a little more than ¾ cup of the butter in a sauté pan over high heat. Add the redfish and cook approximately 8 minutes on each side. Meanwhile, in another pan, melt the remaining butter over low heat and add the lemon juice.

Place the fillets on 6 dinner plates and cover each with about ½ cup of the sautéed crabmeat. Top with the lemon-butter mixture, about 2 tablespoons per portion, and garnish with a lemon star and parsley sprig. Serve immediately.

Redfish Chambord

———————————— *Serves 6* ————————————

This dish, named after the classic French sauce, not the popular liqueur, is unusual in New Orleans because the redfish is poached rather than sautéed or deep-fried.

6 fresh redfish fillets, each approximately 8 ounces
¾ cup Garlic Butter (page 241)
4 cups quartered mushrooms
4½ cups boiled and quartered artichoke bottoms (page 242)
¾ cup Glassage (page 240)
6 parsley sprigs

In a large pot, poach the redfish fillets in 4 quarts boiling water for approximately 12 minutes. They should remain uncrowded in one layer. Two batches may be necessary. When the fillets have about 5 minutes to go, melt the garlic butter in a separate pan over high heat. Add the mushrooms and artichokes to the butter and sauté for about 3 minutes.

When the fillets are cooked, drain them and place on 6 dinner plates. Cover with the mushroom-artichoke mixture and top each with about 2 tablespoons glassage. Place under the broiler until golden brown, only about 10 seconds. Garnish with a parsley sprig and serve immediately.

Redfish Pierre
Serves 6

Departing from the traditional New Orleans style of redfish in a sauce, in this dish the delicacy is coated with Arnaud's special spice blend and bronzed in butter.

½ cup Arnaud Spices (see Note below)
6 fresh redfish fillets, each approximately 7 ounces
4 tablespoons (½ stick) butter
6 lemon stars (see Note on page 132)
6 parsley sprigs

Put the spices in a bowl and dredge the fillets with them. Set aside. Melt 2 tablespoons of the butter in a pan over high heat. As soon as the butter turns brown, add the fillets and cook for 5 minutes on each side.

In the meantime, melt the remaining 2 tablespoons butter in a separate pan. Place the fillets on dinner plates, top with the melted butter, and garnish with a lemon star and parsley sprig. Serve immediately.

NOTE: Though Arnaud's spice blend is the most authentic for the preparation of this recipe, you may substitute any good-quality Creole or Cajun blend.

Flounder John
_____ *Serves 6* _____

Named after the Arnaud's sous-chef who created it, this entrée showcases the delicate local bottom fish in a precise mix of otherwise familiar ingredients. In cooking, as in many things, anyone can put ingredients together, but only a master knows when to stop.

> *6 fresh flounder fillets, each approximately 6 ounces*
> *4 eggs, beaten*
> *4 cups Bread Crumbs Provençale (page 188)*
> *3/4 cup (1 1/2 sticks) butter*
> *3/4 cup Garlic Butter (page 241)*
> *1 1/2 cups boiled and quartered artichoke hearts (page 242)*
> *1 1/2 cups quartered mushrooms*
> *1/4 cup white wine*
> *6 lemon stars (see Note on page 132)*
> *6 parsley sprigs*

Dip the flounder in the eggs, then in the bread crumbs. Melt the butter in a sauté pan over high heat, then add the flounder and cook each fillet about 4 minutes on each side.

In another pan, melt about 1/2 cup of the garlic butter over high heat. Add the artichoke hearts and mushrooms and cook for 3 minutes. Add the wine and cook for 1 minute more.

Place the flounder fillets on dinner plates and cover with the artichoke-mushroom mixture. Top with the remaining garlic butter. Garnish with a lemon star and parsley sprig. Serve immediately.

Frog Legs Provençale
Serves 6

It was decided early on that a restaurant with Arnaud's respect for French tradition needed at least one dish showcasing frog legs. This presentation imaginatively blends the tastes of garlic and Herbsaint.

> *48 medium frog legs, fresh or frozen*
> *Salt and white pepper*
> *$1/2$ cup flour*
> *$1/2$ cup Garlic Butter (page 241)*
> *$1/4$ cup Herbsaint liqueur*
> *$1/4$ cup finely chopped garlic*
> *$1/4$ cup chopped fresh parsley*
> *6 lemon stars (see Note on page 132)*
> *6 parsley sprigs*

Season the frog legs to taste with salt and white pepper, then sprinkle lightly with the flour and shake off any excess. Melt about two-thirds of the garlic butter in a pan over low heat, then add the frog legs and cook until lightly brown. Pour off any excess butter.

Add the Herbsaint and flame, either by tilting the pan carefully over a gas flame or igniting the liquid with a long match. Allow the flames to burn out, and keep the frog legs warm.

In a small pan, melt the remaining garlic butter and add the chopped garlic. Remove from heat. Place 8 frog legs on each of 6 dinner plates. Pour the garlic butter over each portion and sprinkle with the chopped parsley. Garnish the portions with the lemon stars and parsley sprigs. Serve immediately.

Fowl

Chicken Creole

This distinctly Creole dish is made special with a peppy sauce of tomatoes and green peppers.

>   *¹/₄ cup olive oil*
>   *6 boneless chicken breasts, each 5–6 ounces*
>   *1 cup white wine*
>   *4³/₄ cups Creole Sauce (page 227)*

5 cups cooked White Rice (page 200)
1 pinch of chopped parsley

Preheat the oven to 350 degrees.

Heat the oil in a cast-iron skillet over high heat, then add the chicken and sauté each side for about 2 minutes, until golden. Add the white wine and then stir in the Creole sauce. Transfer the mixture to a baking dish or place the skillet in the oven and bake for 7 minutes.

Spoon about ¾ cup of cooked rice onto one side of each dinner plate. Place the chicken breast on the other side and cover with about ¾ cup of the Creole sauce. Garnish by sprinkling the chopped parsley over the chicken. Serve immediately.

Chicken au Vin Rouge
Serves 6

Many Creole-French dishes are notable for their simplicity—but this version of the classic coq au vin is not one of them. Yet the splendid taste amply repays both the time and trouble. Remember to start a day ahead of time, as the chicken must marinate for 24 hours before cooking.

2 quarts red wine
2½ cups sliced carrots (about 5 carrots)
3⅓ cups sliced onions (about 3 large onions)
1⅔ cups sliced celery (about 3 stalks)
2 cloves garlic
1 bay leaf
1 pinch of dried whole thyme
½ teaspoon black peppercorns
1 clove
3 small whole chickens (2½–3 pounds), quartered
Salt and freshly ground black pepper
1½ cups flour, approximately

1¹/₃ cups (2²/₃ sticks) butter
2 quarts Veal Stock (page 237)
1¹/₃ cups quartered mushrooms (about ¹/₂ pound)
4 ounces smoked salt pork, cut up and blanched in water
(see Note below)
1 cup pearl onions, blanched
1 teaspoon sugar
6 slices of homemade or good quality white bread, toasted
and cut diagonally into 12 triangles
¹/₄ cup chopped fresh parsley

Prepare a marinade in a deep dish or roasting pan by combining the red wine, carrots, onions, celery, garlic, bay leaf, thyme, peppercorns, and clove. Add the chicken quarters and marinate, covered, in the refrigerator for 24 hours or more.

When ready to prepare the dish, remove the chicken and strain the marinade. Reserve the vegetables and marinade in separate bowls. Pat the chicken dry and season it with salt and pepper to taste, then sprinkle lightly with flour.

Melt ½ cup of the butter in a large ovenproof casserole over high heat. Add the chicken and sauté until browned, about 4 minutes on each side. Add additional butter as needed. Remove and set aside. Add additional butter as needed. Remove and set aside. Add the reserved vegetables and cook for 8 to 10 minutes over high heat, stirring frequently. Sprinkle the vegetables with ¼ cup of flour and mix well in the pan. Cook over low heat, stirring constantly, to cook the flour and smooth the mixture. Add ½ of the reserved marinade and bring to a boil. Cook over high heat until thickened and reduced by half. Preheat the oven to 350 degrees.

Return the chicken to the casserole, add the veal stock, and cover. Bake in the preheated oven for 25 minutes. While the chicken is in the oven, prepare the rest of the ingredients.

Melt 2 tablespoons of the remaining butter in a pan over high heat, then add the mushrooms and sauté for 5 minutes. Remove from the burner and set aside in a warm place.

Melt another 2 tablespoons of the butter in a pan over high heat. Add the salt pork and sauté for about 2 minutes. Remove from the burner and keep warm with the mushrooms.

Melt the last 2 tablespoons of the butter in a pan over high heat. Add the pearl onions and sauté for 2 minutes, sprinkling with the sugar while sautéing to caramelize them. Remove the pearl onions with a slotted spoon. Set aside with the mushrooms and salt pork.

When the chicken has finished cooking, remove it from the casserole. Strain the sauce, wipe out the casserole and return the sauce. Boil gently for 5 minutes. Add the mushrooms, pork, and onions and simmer for 2 minutes. Add the chicken and simmer for another 2 minutes. Place 2 pieces of the chicken on each dinner plate and cover with the sauce. Garnish with 2 toast triangles. Sprinkle with the chopped parsley and serve.

NOTE: This process, which produces the *lardons* used in traditional French cuisine, is aimed at keeping the pork from drying out as well as lessening its salt content. It is accomplished by cutting the pork ¼ to ½ inch thick and 1 inch long, then boiling it in water for 1 to 2 minutes. Remove the meat with a slotted spoon.

Chicken Rochambeau
Serves 6

This dish reflects the native New Orleanian's love of rich sauces, with not one but two drawing attention here. The Bordelaise and béarnaise, if prepared according to these simple instructions, should remain separate until the first forkful—making for a smashing presentation.

6 boneless chicken breasts, each 5–6 ounces
½ cup white wine
¼ cup finely chopped shallots
3 cups hot Bordelaise Sauce (page 226)
6 Holland Rusks or English muffins
6 slices Canadian bacon, sautéed in butter
1½ cups hot Béarnaise Sauce (page 224)

6 cherry tomatoes
6 parsley sprigs

Preheat the oven to 350 degrees.

Place the chicken breasts in an ovenproof pot and add enough water to cover. Add the wine and shallots and bring to a boil. Place the pot and its contents in the oven, cooking for 8 minutes.

Ladle approximately ½ cup of the Bordelaise sauce on each of 6 dinner plates. Center the Holland Rusk or English muffin in each pool of sauce and cover with a slice of sautéed Canadian bacon. Place a chicken breast on the bacon and carefully pour about ¼ cup of the béarnaise sauce over each. Garnish each with a cherry tomato and a parsley sprig. Serve immediately

Chicken Victoria
———————————— Serves 6 ————————————

This high-style brunch entrée features Arnaud's famous stuffing. The sauce mixes raisins and brandy with a creation based on port wine.

6 boneless chicken breasts, each approximately 5 ounces
3 cups Stuffing (page 165)
6 slices Canadian bacon
Parchment paper
2 cups Veal Stock (page 237)
1 cup raisins
¼ cup brandy
3 cups Port Wine Sauce (page 177)
6 parsley sprigs

Preheat the oven to 350 degrees.

Place the chicken breasts on a work surface, skin side down. Center ½ cup of the stuffing on top of each chicken breast. Fold the sides up over the stuffing and cover with a bacon slice. Wrap each breast around its middle with a ¾-inch-wide strip of parchment paper to help it retain its shape during cooking. Place the breasts in a roasting pan and bake for 45 minutes.

During the final 5 to 7 minutes of cooking time, prepare the sauce. Mix the raisins and brandy in a pan and heat over high heat, then flame. Add the port wine sauce to the pan and bring to a boil. Remove the chicken from the oven when done. Set the breasts on 6 warmed dinner plates and cover each breast with ½ cup of sauce. Garnish each plate with a parsley sprig and serve.

Chicken au Citron
Serves 6

Cuisines east and west have long celebrated the marriage of chicken and lemon. Arnaud's offers one of the most successful variations to be found.

> *6 boneless chicken breasts, each approximately 5 ounces*
> *½ cup white wine*
> *1 cup lemon juice*
> *2 tablespoons finely chopped shallots*
> *4 tablespoons (½ stick) butter*
> *6 parsley sprigs*

To marinate the chicken, use a pan large enough to allow the breasts to lie flat and separate. Combine the white wine, ½ cup of the lemon juice, and the shallots, then pour over the chicken. Marinate for about one hour at room temperature, turning several times. Then remove and broil until done, 6 to 8 minutes.

In the meantime, prepare the lemon butter by melting the butter in a pan over high heat. Add the remaining ½ cup of lemon juice and mix well. Center the chicken breasts on each of 6 dinner plates and cover with the lemon butter. Garnish each with a parsley sprig and serve.

Chicken Chasseur
Serves 6

The scallopini sauce created for Arnaud's famous veal dinner dish turns up at brunch over a boneless chicken breast. And between bursts of jazz and sips of Creole cocktails, guests are voicing their gratitude.

> *4 tablespoons (½ stick) butter*
> *2 teaspoons dried tarragon*
> *6 boneless chicken breasts, each approximately 5 ounces*
> *3 cups Scallopini Sauce (page 175)*
> *6 cherry tomatoes*
> *6 parsley sprigs*

Melt the butter in a large skillet over high heat. Add the tarragon, then add the chicken breasts and sauté on both sides until done, 6 to 8 minutes.

In the meantime, heat the scallopini sauce. Center the chicken breasts on each of 6 dinner plates and cover each with approximately ½ cup of the sauce. Garnish each plate with a cherry tomato and parsley sprig and serve immediately.

Chicken Dijon
Serves 6

A popular item at Arnaud's jazz brunch, this dish weds an elegant boneless chicken breast with the pungent taste of France's best-known mustard.

> *6 boneless chicken breasts, each approximately 8 ounces*
> *½ cup Dijon mustard*

2 cups unseasoned bread crumbs
4 tablespoons (1/2 stick) butter, melted
1 1/4 cups Mustard Sauce (recipe below)
6 parsley sprigs

Preheat the oven to 375 degrees.

Brush both sides of the chicken breasts with Dijon mustard, then cover the top side of the breast with a heavy coating of bread crumbs.

Brush a roasting pan with the melted butter and place the breasts on it (bread crumb side up). Bake for 25 minutes, until cooked through and browned on top. To serve, ladle 1/4 cup mustard sauce on each of 6 dinner plates, top with a chicken breast, decorate with a parsley sprig, and serve.

Mustard Sauce

Yields about 2 cups

1 tablespoon butter
1/8 cup chopped shallots
1/4 cup white wine
2 1/2 cups heavy cream
1 bay leaf
1 1/2 tablespoons cornstarch
1/3 cup Dijon mustard
Salt and freshly ground black pepper

Melt the butter in a pot over high heat, then add the shallots and cook until translucent. Add the white wine and boil for 2 minutes. Add the cream and bay leaf and return to a boil. Reduce the heat and simmer for 2 minutes.

Dissolve the cornstarch in an equal amount of water and add

it gradually until the sauce coats a spoon. Strain, then stir in the mustard with salt and pepper to taste.

NOTE: Mustard sauce can be kept in the refrigerator for 2 to 3 days.

Stuffed Quail au Chambertin
——————————— Serves 6 ———————————

Named after the lovely French wine, this dish is made at Arnaud's with fresh Louisiana quail. The hardest tasks are deboning the quail (buy it deboned if you possibly can) and stuffing it to regain its natural shape. The latter, of course, is hardly make or break—but it certainly spices up the presentation.

> *12 boneless quail, each approximately 3 ounces*
> *3 cups Stuffing (recipe below)*
> *Parchment paper*
> *³/4 cup Chambertin or other red Burgundy wine*
> *1¹/2 cups Bordelaise Sauce (page 226)*
> *3 cups sliced mushrooms*
> *¹/4 cup chopped fresh parsley*

Preheat the oven to 400 degrees.

Stuff each quail with ¼ cup of stuffing and shape with your fingers until it looks like a quail. To help these creations keep their shape during cooking, skirt each snugly with a 2-inch-wide folded strip of parchment paper.

Place the quail in a roasting pan, then add the red wine mixed with 2 tablespoons of the Bordelaise sauce. Cover with aluminum foil and bake in the oven for 20 minutes. Remove the quail from the roasting pan and keep it warm.

Pour the sauce from the roasting pan into a sauté pan or Windsor pan and reduce to one-third its volume on top of the stove over high heat, about 4 minutes. Add the remaining Bordelaise sauce and the sliced mushrooms. Bring to a boil, then reduce the heat and simmer for 3 minutes.

Place 2 quail on each of 6 dinner plates, cover with the sauce, and sprinkle with the chopped parsley. Serve immediately.

Stuffing
Yields 3 cups

8 ounces pork loin
10 ounces veal shank
5 ounces chicken livers
2 tablespoons chopped shallots
$^{1}\!/_{2}$ teaspoon white pepper
$^{1}\!/_{2}$ teaspoon black pepper
$^{1}\!/_{2}$ teaspoon allspice
2 tablespoons chopped fresh parsley
1 egg
2 tablespoons heavy cream
$^{1}\!/_{2}$ teaspoon salt
2 tablespoons port wine

Place the meats in a food processor and process at high speed until the mixture has the consistency of a paste. Transfer the paste to a large bowl and blend in the remaining ingredients by hand.

Refrigerate until ready to use.

NOTE: Stuffing can be kept in the refrigerator for up to 2 days.

Breast of Duck Ellen
_____ Serves 6 _____

This popular dish was named after Archie Casbarian's mother. The real flavor secret is Arnaud's own blueberry vinegar. The boneless duck breasts are glazed in the vinegar, finished with port wine, and garnished with fresh blueberries. Plan to begin this dish the day before serving since the duck must marinate for 24 hours.

> _6 boneless duck breasts, each approximately 10 ounces_
> _2 quarts vegetable oil_
> _2½ cups sliced carrots (about 5 carrots)_
> _2 cups sliced leeks (about 2 leeks)_
> _2⅔ cups sliced onions (about 2 large onions)_
> _1 Bouquet Garni (page 231)_
> _2⅔ cups sliced celery (about 2 ribs)_
> _½ teaspoon black peppercorns_
> _4 tablespoons (½ stick) butter_
> _¼ cup homemade Blueberry Vinegar (recipe below) or good-
>   quality store-bought blueberry vinegar_
> _¼ cup port wine_
> _1½ cups Blueberry Sauce (recipe below)_
> _¾ cup fresh blueberries_
> _Salt and freshly ground black pepper_
> _1 tablespoon chopped fresh parsley_
> _6 parsley sprigs_

Trim each breast and remove approximately half the fat. In a deep dish or roasting pan, make the marinade by combining the oil, carrots, leeks, onions, bouquet garni, celery, and peppercorns. Add the duck breasts and marinate, covered, in the refrigerator for 24 hours. Remove the duck breasts and dry them with paper towels. Discard the marinade.

Melt the butter in a pan over high heat. Add the duck breasts and sauté until pink, about 2½ minutes per side. Remove the breasts and keep warm.

Pour off the grease from the pan, then add the blueberry vinegar and port wine. Reduce the liquid over high heat to one-third its volume, about 3 minutes. Add the blueberry sauce and fresh blueberries. Bring to a boil, then reduce the heat and simmer for 2 minutes. Season to taste with salt and pepper.

Slice each breast into ¼-inch-wide slices, and place each on a dinner plate. Cover with the sauce and sprinkle with the chopped parsley. Garnish with a parsley sprig and serve immediately.

Blueberry Vinegar
Yields 1 quart

1 quart red wine vinegar
2 bay leaves
2 cloves
1 cup fresh blueberries

Bring the vinegar to a boil over high heat, then reduce the heat, add the bay leaves and cloves, and simmer for 10 minutes. Add the blueberries and simmer for 3 minutes.

Remove from the heat, allow to cool to room temperature, then refrigerate uncovered (to speed the chilling process).

NOTE: Covered with plastic wrap, or bottled, this vinegar can keep up to 2 weeks if refrigerated.

Blueberry Sauce
Yields about 2 cups

3 cups Duck Stock (page 236)
1/2 cup blueberries, fresh or frozen
1/4 cup port wine
1/8 cup granulated sugar
1/8 cup red wine vinegar
1/2 cup Blueberry Vinegar (recipe above)
1/4 cup Roux (page 232)
Salt and freshly ground black pepper

Place the duck stock in a pot and reduce by half over high heat, about 8 to 10 minutes. Add the blueberries and port wine, and simmer for 5 minutes.

In the meantime, prepare a caramel in a separate pan as follows. Mix the sugar and 1 teaspoon water thoroughly, then bring to a boil over high heat. Cook until the sugar turns brown, then quickly add the red wine vinegar, being careful not to splash the mixture onto yourself. Add the caramel carefully to the reduced stock.

Boil the mixture for 1 minute before adding the blueberry vinegar. Place the sauce in a blender and blend at high speed for 1 minute, then return it to the pot and bring to a boil. Thicken with the roux, one tablespoon at a time, until it coats a spoon. Season to taste with salt and pepper.

NOTE: Blueberry sauce can be kept, covered, in the refrigerator for up to 1 week.

Roast Duck Mitchell

Named after the same attorney whose last name is showcased in Scallops Hoffman, this is a simple dish that celebrates Louisiana's love of hunting. There is nothing here that could not be done at a dozen wintry duck camps along any stretch of bayou—it's just done better at Arnaud's.

> *3 ducks, each approximately 3 pounds*
> *Salt and freshly ground black pepper*
> *½ cup (1 stick) butter, melted*
> *1 cup honey*
> *½ cup red wine vinegar*
> *6 cherry tomatoes*
> *6 parsley sprigs*

Preheat the oven to 425 degrees.

Season the ducks with salt and pepper to taste and place them in a roasting pan. Brush the exposed surfaces of the birds with the melted butter, then slip the pan into the oven and bake for 30 minutes.

Remove the ducks from the oven and cut each in quarters. Reduce the oven temperature to 325 degrees, set the duck quarters in a large skillet, cover them with honey, and return to the oven for 6 minutes. Transfer 2 duck quarters to each of 6 warmed dinner plates.

Place the skillet over high heat, pour in the vinegar and bring to a boil. Pour this sauce over the duck quarters. Garnish each plate with a cherry tomato and a parsley sprig. Serve immediately.

Roast Duck à L'Orange
Serves 6

In this dish—one of the true classics of old France—orange zest, orange sauce, and orange wedges join forces to showcase the simply but carefully roasted ducks.

> *3 whole ducks, each approximately 4 pounds*
> *1¼ cups (2½ sticks) butter*
> *2½ cups sliced carrots (about 5 carrots)*
> *3 medium onions, sliced*
> *1 Bouquet Garni (page 231)*
> *1 clove garlic*
> *½ cup granulated sugar*
> *4 tablespoons slivered orange zest*
> *2¼ cups Orange Sauce (recipe below)*
> *¼ cup chopped fresh parsley*
> *6 circular orange slices (1 orange)*
> *18 orange wedges (3 oranges)*
> *6 parsley sprigs*

Preheat the oven to 375 degrees. Place the ducks in a roasting pan and rub the butter over their exposed surfaces. Add the carrots, onions, bouquet garni, and garlic to the pan. Bake in the oven for 1¼ hours.

Discard the vegetables. Remove the ducks from the pan, halve them, and carefully remove all the bones and cartilage from the breasts, along with the skin and excess fat from all the pieces. Bones can remain in the wings and legs. Keep the ducks warm.

Combine the sugar with 1 cup water in a pot and bring to a boil over high heat. Add the orange zest and cook for 1 minute. Strain the zest carefully.

Place the duck halves on dinner plates, sprinkle with the orange zest, cover with the orange sauce, and sprinkle with the chopped parsley. Garnish each serving with 1 orange slice, 3 orange wedges, and a parsley sprig. Serve immediately.

Orange Sauce
Yields 1 quart

6 cups Duck Stock (page 236)
1 orange, sliced
1 lemon, sliced
1 Bouquet Garni (page 231)
1 6-ounce can frozen orange juice, defrosted
1/4 cup Grand Marnier liqueur
1/3 cup granulated sugar
1/2 cup white wine vinegar
3–4 tablespoons Roux (page 232)
Salt and freshly ground black pepper

In a pot over high heat, reduce the duck stock by one-third. Add the orange, lemon, bouquet garni, orange juice, and Grand Marnier, then bring to a boil.

In the meantime, prepare a caramel as follows: in a separate pot, mix the sugar and 2 tablespoons water very well. Bring to a boil over high heat and keep cooking until it becomes a thick, light-brown mixture. While stirring, slowly add the vinegar, being careful not to splash any of the molten mixture on yourself.

Add the caramel immediately to the duck stock mixture and boil for 2 minutes. Thicken, gradually adding small amounts of roux until the sauce coats a spoon. Strain through a strainer and season to taste with salt and pepper.

NOTE: Orange sauce can be kept, covered, in the refrigerator for up to 1 week.

Twelfth Night Cornish Game Hen
Serves 6

Germaine Wells, the Count's only daughter and his successor at Arnaud's, expressed her passionate love of New Orleans' Carnival celebration with this notable dish. In Christian tradition, Twelfth Night is the final fling of the Christmas season. In New Orleans, it is also the first fling of Carnival.

> *6 boneless Cornish hens, each approximately 8 ounces*
> *2¾ cups Cornish Hen Stuffing (recipe below)*
> *Parchment paper*
> *1 cup red wine*
> *1¼ cups Bordelaise Sauce (page 226)*
> *1¼ cups Veal Stock (page 237)*
> *3 cups quartered mushrooms (about 1 pound)*
> *2 cups diced tomatoes (about 4 tomatoes)*
> *¼ cup chopped fresh parsley*
> *6 parsley sprigs*

Preheat the oven to 400 degrees.

Stuff each hen with just under ½ cup stuffing and shape to look like the original small bird. To help the hen keep its shape during cooking, wrap with a snug 2-inch-wide strip of parchment paper. Place the hens in a roasting pan.

Add the red wine, ¼ cup of the Bordelaise sauce, the veal stock, mushrooms, and tomatoes. Cover with aluminum foil and bake for 40 minutes. Remove the hens and keep them warm.

Pour the sauce from the roasting pan into a saucepan and reduce by one-third over high heat, about 4 minutes. Add the remaining cup of Bordelaise sauce, bring to a boil, and reduce the heat. Simmer for 5 minutes. Place each hen on a dinner plate and cover with sauce. Sprinkle with the chopped parsley, garnish with a parsley sprig, and serve immediately.

Cornish Hen Stuffing
_____ *Yields 2³/₄ cups* _____

7 ounces veal, minced
7 ounces pork, minced
4 ounces chicken livers, minced
4 eggs
¼ cup heavy cream
Salt and freshly ground black pepper
2 tablespoons brandy
2 tablespoons marsala wine
1 cup chopped fresh parsley

Place all the ingredients in a mixing bowl and mix at medium speed until the stuffing is smooth. Cover with plastic wrap and refrigerate until needed.

NOTE: The stuffing can be kept refrigerated up to 2 days.

Meats

Veal Scallopini Gille

Serves 6

Named after Arnaud's executive chef, this veal dish draws most of its appeal from its sauce—a luscious mix of tomatoes and mushrooms with white, red, and marsala wines, thickened with a classic roux.

> _6 top-quality baby veal slices, each approximately 4 ounces_
> _½ cup flour_
> _Salt and freshly ground black pepper_

6 tablespoons (3/4 stick) butter
1 1/2 cups Scallopini Sauce (recipe below)
1 cup chopped green onions or scallions

Dredge the veal slices on both sides with the flour and shake off any excess. Season to taste with salt and pepper. Melt the butter in a pan over low heat, then add the veal and sauté about 1 minute on each side.

Place the veal slices on dinner plates and cover with the scallopini sauce, approximately 1/4 cup per serving. Sprinkle with the green onions or scallions and serve immediately.

Scallopini Sauce
Yields about 2 cups

This sauce is wonderful over an omelette, as well as over veal.

1 tablespoon butter
2 tablespoons cup chopped shallots
1/8 cup chopped green onions or scallions
1/4 cup sliced mushrooms
1 Bouquet Garni (page 231)
1/4 cup diced fresh tomatoes, with the liquid squeezed out
1/2 teaspoon chopped garlic
1/4 cup red wine
1/8 cup white wine
1 tablespoon marsala wine
1 1/2 cups Veal Stock (page 237)
6 tablespoons Roux (page 232)
Salt and freshly ground black pepper

Melt the butter in a pot over high heat. Add the shallots and green onions, or scallions, and cook until translucent, then add the mushrooms and cook for 2 minutes more. Add the bouquet garni, diced tomatoes, and garlic. Pour in the red wine, white wine, and marsala, and reduce the liquid by half over high heat.

Add the veal stock and bring to a boil, then reduce the heat and simmer for 10 minutes. Gradually thicken with small amounts of the roux until the sauce coats a spoon. Season to taste with salt and pepper. Remove the bouquet garni.

NOTE: Scallopini sauce can be kept, covered, in the refrigerator for up to 1 week.

Veal Wohl
Serves 6

Arnaud's created this dish for those diners who can't quite decide between crawfish and crabmeat as a topping for their veal. So, lump crabmeat covers one side of each veal slice, while Crawfish O'Connor covers the other.

> *6 top-quality baby veal slices, each approximately 3 ounces*
> *1/2 cup flour*
> *Salt and freshly ground black pepper*
> *6 tablespoons (3/4 stick) butter*
> *3/4 cup Sautéed Crabmeat (page 232)*
> *1 1/4 cups Crawfish O'Connor (page 142)*
> *1 1/4 cups Port Wine Sauce (recipe below)*
> *1/4 cup chopped fresh parsley*
> *6 cherry tomatoes*

Dredge each slice of veal in flour. Shake off any excess and season to taste with salt and pepper. Melt the butter in a pan over high heat, then add the veal and sauté approximately 1 minute on each side.

Place a slice of veal in the center of each of 6 dinner plates. Place approximately 2 tablespoons of sautéed crabmeat on one side of each slice and 2 liberal tablespoons of Crawfish O'Connor on the other side.

Top the entire presentation with 2 liberal tablespoons of port wine sauce. Sprinkle with the parsley, garnish with the cherry tomatoes, and serve.

Port Wine Sauce
_____ Yields about 2 cups _____

⅛ cup chopped shallots
1 Bouquet Garni (page 231)
2½ cups port wine
1 cup Veal Stock (page 237)
3 tablespoons Roux (page 232)
Salt and freshly ground black pepper

Heat a saucepan over high heat until drops of water crackle when added. Add the shallots, bouquet garni, and port wine, then keep the heat high and reduce the liquid to one-third volume.

Add the veal stock and bring to a boil. Reduce the heat and simmer for 10 minutes. Thicken gradually with small amounts of the roux until the sauce coats a spoon. Season to taste with salt and pepper.

NOTE: Port wine sauce can be kept, covered, in the refrigerator for up to 1 week.

Veal Lafitte
Serves 6

Archie Casbarian named this dish after his and his adopted city's favorite pirate—Jean Lafitte, hero with Andrew Jackson at the Battle of New Orleans. The sauce, based on veal stock and boasting quartered artichoke bottoms, is enlivened by sherry and both red and white vermouth.

> 6 top-quality baby veal slices, each approximately 4 ounces
> 1/2 cup flour
> Salt and freshly ground black pepper
> 6 tablespoons (3/4 stick) butter
> 1 1/2 cups Lafitte Sauce (recipe below)
> 1/4 cup chopped fresh parsley

Dredge the veal slices in flour on both sides and shake off any excess, then season to taste with salt and pepper. Melt the butter in a pan over low heat, then add the veal and sauté approximately 1 minute on each side.

Place each veal slice on a dinner plate and cover each with about 1/4 cup Lafitte sauce. Sprinkle with the parsley and serve.

Lafitte Sauce
Yields about 2 cups

In addition to its use in Veal Laffite, this sauce is also excellent over poached chicken.

> 2 tablespoons (1/4 stick) butter
> 1/8 cup finely chopped shallots
> 1/4 cup finely chopped green onions or scallions

1 Bouquet Garni (page 231)
1 tablespoon sherry
½ cup red vermouth
¼ cup white vermouth
½ cup heavy cream
½ cup Veal Stock (page 237)
1 tablespoon cornstarch
¼ head Boston lettuce, shredded
2 cups artichoke hearts, boiled, rinsed, and quartered (page 242)
Salt and freshly ground black pepper

Melt the butter in a large saucepan over high heat. Add the shallots and green onions, or scallions, cooking until translucent. Then add the bouquet garni, sherry, and red and white vermouth. Reduce to one-third volume over high heat, about 10 minutes.

Add the cream and bring to a boil, then add the veal stock and return to a boil. Reduce the heat and simmer for 7 minutes. In a small bowl, mix the cornstarch with an equal amount of water and add this gradually in small amounts to thicken the sauce until it coats a spoon.

Add the shredded lettuce and quartered artichoke hearts. Simmer for 3 minutes, then season to taste with salt and pepper. Remove the bouquet garni.

NOTE: Lafitte Sauce can be kept, covered, in the refrigerator for up to 3 days.

Grillades and Grits
Serves 6

When it's time for brunch, it's hard to get more Creole than this traditional recipe. Arnaud's here serves up its popular version.

*18 thin slices top-quality baby veal, each approximately 1
    ounce*
½ cup flour
½ cup (1 stick) butter
3 cups cooked grits
¾ cup Creole Sauce (page 227)
¾ cup Bordelaise Sauce (page 226)
2 teaspoons chopped fresh parsley

Dredge the slices of veal in the flour, shaking off any excess. Melt the butter in a large pan over high heat, then add the veal and sauté about 1 minute on each side. Remove the veal and keep it warm.

Place both sauces in the pan and cook for 1 minute, stirring gently. Place the veal on one side of 6 dinner plates and the grits on the other. Cover each veal serving with ¼ cup of the sauce, sprinkle with the chopped parsley, and serve immediately.

Steak au Poivre
_____ *Serves 6* _____

While far from an Arnaud's original, this dish continues to be a source of great pride around the restaurant's kitchen. Aficionados say Arnaud's sauce is what sets this version apart.

6 prime-grade tenderloin filets, each approximately 8 ounces
Coarsely ground black peppercorns
Salt
¼ cup (½ stick) butter
¼ cup brandy
1¼ cups cream
1 cup Veal Stock (page 237)
6 parsley sprigs

Preheat the oven to 350 degrees.

Gently press cracked peppercorns to taste into both sides of each filet with the flat side of a mallet or chopper and add salt to taste.

Melt the butter in an ovenproof pan over high heat, then add the filets and sear on each side. Remove the pan from the burner and place it in the oven, cooking the filets to the desired degree of doneness (see Note below). Remove the pan from the oven and pour off the remaining butter.

Add the brandy and ignite, either by tilting the hot pan over a stove-top flame or lighting it carefully with a long match. When the flames have burned out, add the cream and reduce the liquid by half over high heat. Add the veal stock and reduce the sauce until it coats a spoon. Season with additional salt if desired.

Place each filet on a dinner plate and cover with the sauce. Garnish with a parsley sprig and serve immediately.

NOTE: Here is Arnaud's guide to achieving the desired degree of doneness when using filets of prime-grade tenderloin approximately 3 inches thick. Preheat the oven to 350 degrees. Rare should be cooked 6 minutes on each side, medium rare 7–8 minutes, medium 8–9 minutes, and well-done 10 minutes.

Filet Mignon Charlemond
Serves 6

This Casbarian dish pledges allegiance to the French flag with its two-colored sauce. The result is a dramatic dish with lots of eye appeal.

> *6 prime-grade tenderloin filets, each approximately 8 ounces*
> *Salt and freshly ground black pepper*
> *¼ cup (½ stick) butter*
> *2 cups Charlemond Sauce (recipe below)*

³/₄ cup Béarnaise Sauce (page 224)
6 parsley sprigs

Preheat the boiler.

Season the filets with salt and pepper to taste. Melt the butter and brush each filet with it, then cook under the broiler to desired doneness (see Note of previous recipe).

Place each cooked filet on a dinner plate and cover each with about ⅓ cup hot Charlemond sauce, then top each with about 2 tablespoons béarnaise sauce. Garnish with a parsley sprig and serve.

Charlemond Sauce

Yields about 2 cups

This wonderful sauce is used at Arnaud's to top the filet of the same name. At home, it's a fine way to dress up a steak on short notice.

1 tablespoon butter
1¹/₂ teaspoons chopped shallots
³/₄ cup chopped green onions or scallions
3 cups sliced mushrooms
1 Bouquet Garni (page 231)
¹/₂ teaspoon chopped garlic
¹/₈ cup white wine
1¹/₂ teaspoons chicken base or dehydrated bouillon
¹/₂ cup milk
¹/₂ cup heavy cream
1 tablespoon Roux (page 232)
Salt and freshly ground black pepper

Melt the butter in a pot over high heat, then add the shallots and green onions, or scallions, and cook until translucent. Add the mushrooms and cook for 3 minutes. Add the bouquet garni and garlic, followed by the white wine and chicken base. Continue cooking for 1 minute.

Add the milk and cream and bring to a boil, then reduce the heat and simmer for 5 minutes. Remove the bouquet garni. Thicken the sauce by gradually adding the roux until the sauce coats a spoon. Season to taste with salt and pepper.

NOTE: Charlemond Sauce can be kept, covered, in the refrigerator for up to 1 week.

Filet Périgourdine
Serves 6

A sophisticated French classic for diners who love beef but demand more than a simple steak, this dish glories in the two most famous products of the Périgord. The goose liver pâté should be purchased with truffles, and search out the freshest possible additional truffles for the heavenly sauce. This dish is expensive, but definitely worth it for special occasions.

> 6 prime-grade tenderloin filets, each approximately 8 ounces
> 6 tablespoons (¾ stick) butter, melted
> Salt and freshly ground black pepper
> 3 tablespoons (6 ounces) goose liver pâté with truffles
> 1 tablespoon chopped fresh truffles
> 1½ cups Port Wine Sauce (page 177)
> 6 parsley sprigs

Heat the butter in a pan over high heat. Add the filets and sauté, turning every 2 minutes until they reach desired doneness (14 minutes for rare, 16 for medium rare, 18 for medium, 22 for well-done). Season to taste with salt and pepper and place each on a dinner plate.

Top each filet with ½ tablespoon of goose liver pâté with

truffles. Mix the additional truffles with the hot port wine sauce and ladle approximately ¼ cup over each filet. Garnish with the parsley sprigs and serve immediately.

Sirloin Steak Maitre D'
Serves 6

New Orleans has a long-standing passion for beef with butter—in this case a distinctive version whipped up in honor of the maitre d'. Even steak purists should respond enthusiastically to this preparation.

6 prime-grade sirloin steaks, each approximately 9 ounces
¾ cup (1½ sticks) butter, melted
Salt and freshly ground black pepper
¾ cup Maitre D' Butter (recipe below)
3 bunches watercress

Preheat the broiler.

Using a pastry brush, brush each steak on both sides with the melted butter. Season to taste with salt and pepper. Place under the broiler and cook until desired doneness (see Note on page 181).

Transfer the steaks to dinner plates and top each with 2 table-spoons of Maitre D' butter. Garnish with the watercress and serve immediately.

Maitre D' Butter
Yields 1 cup

1 cup (2 sticks) unsalted butter
1 bunch fresh parsley, chopped

Juice of 2 fresh lemons
Salt and white pepper

Using a mixer set at low speed, soften the butter, then add the remaining ingredients and mix until well-blended. Season to taste with salt and white pepper. Refrigerate until ready to use.

Beef Wellington
_____ *Serves 6* _____

Here is a dish which, though served all around the world, is given a little extra class at Arnaud's. Added to the menu in the Casbarian era, it is the single most famous beef presentation. And at Arnaud's, each serving is a special fully pastried filet rather than a slice from a larger cut.

6 prime-grade tenderloin filets, each approximately 6 ounces
3¹/₃ cups chopped fresh mushrooms
8 ounces duck or goose liver pâté (sold by weight)
2 tablespoons cognac
Salt and freshly ground black pepper
2 pounds fresh puff pastry, or 3 sheets good-quality frozen
2 eggs, beaten
1¹/₂ cups Port Wine Sauce (page 177)
6 parsley sprigs

Preheat the oven to 350 degrees.

Prepare the mousse by combining the mushrooms, pâté, cognac, and salt and pepper to taste in a food processor or blender. Blend carefully, using on and off turns, until the mixture has the consistency of a thick paste.

Roll the puff pastry ¹/₈ inch thick, then cut out 6 rectangles 6 by 7 inches. Place approximately 3 tablespoons of the mousse on each, spreading evenly. Set aside.

In a heated pan over high heat, sear each filet quickly on both sides. Cool to room temperature. Place each filet on one half of the moussed puff pastry rectangles and cover with an additional 3 table-spoons of the mousse mixture. Brush the edges of the dough with egg.

Fold each square of dough over to seal the filet and mousse, pressing closed with the fingers. Using your imagination, decorate with any remaining puff pastry, perhaps cut into shapes, and brush all exposed surfaces with egg. Bake to the desired degree of done-ness (15 minutes for rare, 19 for medium rare, 23 for medium, and 26 for medium well).

Ladle about ¼ cup of hot port wine sauce on each of 6 dinner plates. Place the pastried filets on the sauce, garnish with the parsley sprigs, and serve immediately.

Tips of Filet en Brochette
———————————— Serves 6 ————————————

The concept of shish kebab spread out from the Middle East, even finding a place in French tradition as any dish cooked *en brochette*. A Creole touch is added by the white rice, used instead of a Turkish or Lebanese pilaf.

> *24 ounces prime-grade tenderloin, cut in 1-inch cubes*
> *12 medium mushroom caps*
> *1 green pepper, cut in 1-inch squares*
> *3 cups hot cooked White Rice (page 200)*
> *2 ¾ cups Bordelaise Sauce (page 226)*
> *¼ cup chopped fresh parsley*

Alternate the meat with the vegetables on 6 skewers and cook under the broiler until done to preference. Place ½ cup hot cooked white rice on each of 6 dinner plates. Top with the kebabs, pull out the skewers, and cover the meat and vegetables with the Bordelaise sauce. Sprinkle with the chopped parsley and serve.

Boiled Brisket of Beef
Serves 6

For all their love of fresh seafood and rich, French-inspired sauces, the old Creoles enjoyed few things as much as a full-flavored beef brisket cooked slowly with vegetables. Here is an unpretentious dish that is a favorite for lunch and for brunch at Arnaud's.

>   3½ pound beef brisket
>   2 cups sliced carrots
>   1 cup sliced leeks
>   1⅓ cups sliced celery
>   1 onion, sliced
>   4 bay leaves
>   6 cloves
>   1 teaspoon black peppercorns
>   1 head cabbage
>   6 medium-sized potatoes
>   2 teaspoons chopped fresh parsley

Place 3 gallons water in a large pot and bring to a boil over high heat, then add the brisket and cook for 10 minutes. Skim any fat from the water, then add the carrots, leeks, celery, onion, bay leaves, cloves, and peppercorns. Bring to a boil, then reduce the heat and simmer for 1½ hours.

In the meantime, clean the cabbage and cut it into 6 wedges. Clean and peel the potatoes.

Remove the brisket from the pot and keep it warm in the oven at 170 degrees. Bring the remaining liquid to a boil and add the cabbage and potatoes. Cook, covered, for 20 minutes. When ready to serve, slice the brisket and place some on each of 6 dinner plates. Garnish with cabbage and potatoes, sprinkle parsley on the potatoes, and serve.

Rack of Lamb Diablo

———————— *Serves 6* ————————

This Arnaud's favorite glows warmly with earthy flavors, from the mustard–bread crumb crust on the rack of lamb to the colorful, flavorful vegetables used as garnish.

> *3 racks of fresh top-quality domestic lamb*
> *¼ cup Dijon mustard*
> *2 cups Bread Crumbs Provençale (recipe below)*
> *Salt and freshly ground black pepper*
> *1 pound broccoli, cooked (page 198)*
> *3 Tomatoes Provençale (page 200)*
> *3 cups Brabant Potatoes (page 196)*

Preheat the oven to 375 degrees.

Place the racks in a roasting pan and sear over high heat on the stovetop for 2 minutes on each side. Remove from the stovetop and roast in the oven for 25 minutes.

Remove and coat each rack with the Dijon mustard, then cover with the bread crumbs. Season to taste with salt and pepper. Return to the oven and bake for 2 minutes, or until the bread crumbs turn golden brown.

Place half a rack on each of 6 dinner plates. Garnish with the broccoli, half a tomato, and Brabant potatoes and serve immediately.

Bread Crumbs Provençale

———————— *Yields about 2 cups* ————————

> *2 cups bread crumbs*
> *⅛ cup finely chopped garlic*

¾ cup finely chopped fresh parsley
½ teaspoon dried basil
½ teaspoon dried marjoram
¼ cup virgin olive oil

In a bowl, mix the bread crumbs, garlic, parsley, basil, and marjoram. Slowly add the olive oil and mix well with a fork. If the bread crumbs are especially dry, you might need additional oil.

Double Lamb Chops Arnaud
———————————————— *Serves 6* ————————————————

Using top-quality double chops is the only secret here, since the lamb chops must stand without a stunning sauce or any eye-catching strokes of restaurant theater.

12 domestic top-quality double lamb chops
¼ cup virgin olive oil
1½ cups Provençale herbs (see Note below)
3 bunches watercress
6 cherry tomatoes

Preheat the broiler.

Dip the lamb chops in olive oil and coat them with the herbs. Spread the chops on a sheet pan and place them under the broiler, cooking for 7 minutes on each side (for medium). Place 2 chops on each of 6 dinner plates, garnish with ½ bunch watercress and a cherry tomato. Serve immediately.

NOTE: For seasoning, you can use a good-quality Provençale herb blend—such as Arnaud's. Or you can prepare your own blend from desired amounts of thyme, basil, rosemary, and garlic powder.

Pork Normande

This delightful brunch selection blends the elemental flavor of pork loin with that of Normandy's favorite taste—apples, represented here not only in their natural form but also in the bracing apple brandy called Calvados.

> *½ cup vegetable oil*
> *6 tablespoons (¾ stick) butter*
> *1 five-pound pork loin*
> *1 cup sliced carrots*
> *1 ⅓ cups sliced white onions*
> *2 quarts Veal Stock (page 237)*
> *2 cups heavy cream*
> *2 teaspoons chopped shallots*
> *¼ cup Calvados*
> *2–3 tablespoons cornstarch*
> *3 apples, peeled, cored, and cut in cubes*
> *Salt and white pepper*
> *1 tablespoon chopped fresh parsley*

Preheat the oven to 400 degrees.

Heat the oil and 4 tablespoons of the butter in a roasting pan over high heat, then add the pork loin, carrots, and onions and sauté for 5 minutes on each side. Place in the oven and cook for 30 minutes. Add the veal stock and cook in the oven for 45 minutes more.

When the pork still has about 15 minutes to go, combine the cream and shallots in a pan and boil for 4 minutes. Add the Calvados and bring to a boil. Reduce the heat and simmer for 3 minutes. Meanwhile, dissolve the cornstarch in an equal amount of water and add this mixture, little by little, to the pan until the sauce is thick enough to coat a spoon.

Melt the remaining 2 tablespoons butter in a separate pan over high heat, then add the cubed apples and sauté for 4 minutes. Strain the apples and add them to the cream sauce. Season to taste with salt and white pepper.

To serve, slice the pork and set the slices on 6 dinner plates. Cover with the sauce, sprinkle with the chopped parsley, and serve.

Tripe à la Mode de Caen

Arnaud's has chosen to serve tripe in its single best-known presentation. The dish hails from coastal Normandy and is named after one of that region's cities.

> *¹/₂ cup (1 stick) butter*
> *¹/₄ cup oil*
> *5 pounds beef tripe, diced*
> *1 whole pig's foot (optional)*
> *2 cups diced carrots*
> *2 cups diced celery*
> *1 Bouquet Garni (page 231)*
> *3 cloves*
> *¹/₂ teaspoon black peppercorns*
> *2 pinches of dried whole thyme*
> *¹/₂ cup diced fresh tomatoes*
> *3 tablespoons tomato purée*
> *¹/₄ cup brandy*
> *1 cup white wine*
> *1 cup marsala wine*
> *3 bay leaves*
> *Salt and freshly ground black pepper*
> *2 tablespoons chopped fresh parsley*

Preheat the oven to 275 degrees.

Heat the butter and oil in a large pot or casserole over high heat. Add the tripe and the pig's foot, if using, and sauté for 7 minutes until browned.

Add the carrots, celery, bouquet garni, cloves, black peppercorns, and thyme and sauté for 4 minutes more. Add the diced tomatoes and tomato purée, followed by the brandy. Flame the brandy either by tilting the pan over a gas flame or igniting the liquid carefully with a long match.

When the flames have burned out, add 2 quarts water, the white wine, marsala, and bay leaves. Bring to a boil, then reduce the heat and simmer for 5 minutes. Cover tightly and cook in the oven for 3 hours. Check every 30 to 40 minutes, replenishing liquid with more water if necessary.

When done, season to taste with salt and pepper. Remove the pig's foot, bay leaves, and bouquet garni. Serve in a soup bowl and decorate with the chopped parsley.

Sweetbreads Eleanor
Serves 6

Named after the proprietor's mother-in-law, this Creole version of a French standard harks back to the earliest days of New Orleans fare. Many restaurants catered to butchers working in the French Market—and featured a wide variety of meat cuts and organs, such as the humble sweetbreads in this elegant presentation with wild mushrooms.

> *2 pounds sweetbreads*
> *Courtbouillon to cover (page 234)*
> *¾ cup (1½ sticks) butter*
> *1 cup chopped shallots*
> *3 tablespoons brandy*
> *1½ cups Bordelaise Sauce (page 226)*
> *4 ½ cups chanterelle mushrooms, or other wild mushrooms*
> *2 tablespoons chopped fresh parsley*
> *6 parsley sprigs*

Cook the sweetbreads in the Courtbouillon for 25 minutes, then remove them with a slotted spoon. Plunge them in cold water, remove any membrane, then slice them.

Melt ½ cup of the butter in a pan over high heat. Add the sweetbreads, followed by about ⅓ cup of the shallots, and sauté until golden, approximately 5 minutes. Pour off the remaining butter, add the brandy, and ignite either by tilting over a gas flame or lighting the liquid carefully with a long match.

When the flames have burned out, add the Bordelaise sauce and bring to a boil. Then reduce the heat and simmer for 3 minutes.

In a separate pan, melt the remaining ¼ cup butter over high heat, add the chanterelle mushrooms, and sauté for 3 minutes. Add the remaining ⅔ cup shallots, mix thoroughly with the chanterelles, sauté 2 minutes more and remove from heat.

Center the sweetbreads mixture on each of 6 dinner plates, then place about 3 tablespoons of chanterelles on each side of the mixture. Sprinkle the sweetbreads with the chopped parsley, garnish with a parsley sprig, and serve.

Vegetables

Creamed Spinach

Serves 6

Nutmeg adds a Creole surprise to this wonderful French standard. Take care to wash the spinach repeatedly to remove any stubborn grit, and deposit the leaves in ice water to maximize their crispness.

6 tablespoons salt
4 10-ounce bags of fresh spinach, or 4 pounds sold loose
½ cup Béchamel Sauce (page 225)

> *½ cup heavy cream*
> *Pinch of nutmeg*
> *Salt and white pepper*

Combine the salt and 4 quarts water in a pot and bring to a boil over high heat. Meanwhile, wash the spinach in water three or four times, changing the water for each dousing, until all grit is washed away. Place the spinach in the boiling water and cook uncovered for 5 minutes. Drain and place in cold water with ice.

Purée the spinach in a blender or food processor. In a pot over low heat, combine the spinach, béchamel sauce, cream, and nutmeg. Make sure all the ingredients are well blended, season to taste with salt and pepper, and serve.

Cauliflower au Gratin
Serves 6

One of Arnaud's most popular vegetable dishes, this one makes a marriage of fresh cauliflower, béchamel sauce, and Swiss cheese.

> *1½ tablespoons salt*
> *1 head cauliflower (approximately 2 pounds)*
> *2 cups Béchamel Sauce (page 225)*
> *1½ cups grated Swiss cheese*

Preheat the oven to 350 degrees.

Combine 4 quarts water and the salt in a large pot and bring to a boil over high heat. Add the cauliflower and cook for 20 minutes. Remove the pot from the heat and place under cold running water, then remove the cauliflower and drain.

Divide the cauliflower among 6 oval ramekins. Cover each with about ⅓ cup béchamel sauce and place in the oven for 5 minutes. Remove, sprinkle with Swiss cheese, and place under the broiler until golden brown, 1 to 2 minutes. Serve immediately.

Brabant Potatoes
————————————— Serves 6 —————————————

Though named after a section of the Low Countries where potatoes have long been grown and survived on, this vegetable dish owes as much to Southern Europe. The bread crumbs Provençale are Arnaud's special addition.

> *Vegetable oil, enough for a deep fryer or 1 inch deep in a*
> *large skillet*
> *4¹/₂ cups potatoes peeled, cubed*
> *1 cup Bread Crumbs Provençale (page 188)*
> *2 tablespoons chopped fresh parsley*
> *Salt and freshly ground black pepper*

Heat the oil to 375 degrees in a large skillet over high heat, or use a deep fryer. Add the potatoes and cook for 8 minutes, until they turn golden brown. Drain them and transfer them to a small roasting pan. Add the bread crumbs, parsley, and salt and pepper to taste. Mix well and serve very hot.

Soufflé Potatoes
————————————— Serves 6 —————————————

The secret to irresistible soufflé potatoes is a special French gadget called the *mandolin,* which makes the necessary thin slices with absolute uniformity. The *mandolin* is available from gourmet cookware shops or from Arnaud's.

> *4 quarts vegetable oil*
> *4 Idaho potatoes*
> *Salt*

Put the oil in a fryer and heat to 300 degrees.

Peel the potatoes and cut the sides to form a rectangle. Using a *mandolin,* slice the potatoes ⅛ inch thick (it is imperative that the thickness be uniform). Wash well and dry.

Place the slices in the hot oil and cook until they float to the surface. Remove them and raise the oil's temperature to the smoking point, about 450 degrees, then return them to the oil and fry until golden brown, dry, and crisp. The potatoes should puff immediately upon their return to the hot oil.

Remove them from the oil, drain on paper towels, and salt lightly. Serve on a napkin-lined dinner plate.

French Fried Potatoes
Serves 6

4 quarts vegetable oil
4 Colorado (or Idaho) potatoes
Salt

Put the oil in a fryer and heat to 400 degrees.

Peel the potatoes and cut the sides to form a rectangle, then cut them with a French fry cutter, wash well, and dry.

Cook in the hot oil until they turn yellow, then remove them and set aside for 5 minutes so the oil can regain its temperature. Return the potatoes to the oil and cook until they are crisp. Remove, drain, and dry on cheesecloth or paper towels. Salt to taste and serve immediately.

Eggplant au Gratin
Serves 6

In search of interesting vegetable dishes, Casbarian embraced this one as yet another showcase for his Middle Eastern roots and his classical European training. The herbs add a Creole dash to the dish, as do the diced tomatoes.

> *1 cup olive oil*
> *3 pounds eggplant, cut in 1-inch cubes*
> *1 cup chopped green onions or scallions (about 1 bunch)*
> *1 teaspoon dried marjoram*
> *1 teaspoon dried thyme*
> *1 teaspoon dried whole sweet basil*
> *2 bay leaves*
> *2 tablespoons chopped garlic*
> *1 cup diced fresh tomatoes*
> *Salt and freshly ground black pepper*
> *¾ cup grated Swiss cheese*

Heat the oil in a pan over high heat, then add the eggplant, followed by the green onions or scallions and all the herbs. Sauté for 4 minutes, then add the garlic and diced tomatoes. Cook this mixture for 5 minutes over low heat. Season to taste with salt and pepper.

Divide the mixture among 6 ramekins and cover with the cheese. Place under the broiler until brown, about 2 minutes, and serve immediately.

Broccoli Hollandaise
Serves 6

This is certainly one of tne loveliest vegetable presentations imaginable. It is the perfect accompaniment for almost any entrée.

3 tablespoons salt
3 bunches broccoli, cleaned
1 cup Hollandaise Sauce (page 228)

Combine the water and salt in a large pot and bring to a boil over high heat. Add the broccoli and cook uncovered (to keep it green) for 12 minutes. Remove the broccoli and drain it, then divide it among 6 plates, top with the hollandaise, and serve.

Julienne of Vegetables
Serves 6

A julienne of vegetables is one of the most delicate ways to accompany an entrée. Arnaud's suggests using a French fry cutter to julienne the carrots, turnips, and zucchini, but a food processor with the proper attachment or a careful hand with a knife works equally well. Each vegetable is cooked separately because each needs a different length of cooking time.

1/2 pound carrots
1/3 pound turnips
1/3 pound zucchini
3/8 cup salt
2/3 stick butter
Salt and freshly ground black pepper
2 teaspoons chopped fresh parsley

Cut the vegetables into julienne strips, approximately 2 inches long, 1/4 inch wide, and 1/4 inch thick. Place 4 quarts of water and 1/8 cup of the salt into each of 3 pots and bring to a boil over high heat. Add a vegetable to each pot, and cook the carrots for 6 minutes, the turnips for 4 minutes, and the zucchini for 3 minutes.

When the vegetables are done, place the pots under cold running water until the contents are cold. Pour all the vegetables into a single large colander and drain.

Melt the butter in a pan over high heat, then add the vegetable mixture and sauté for 4 to 5 minutes. Season to taste with salt and pepper, then add the parsley. Divide among 6 small plates and serve immediately.

Tomatoes Provençale
Serves 6

Here is Arnaud's formula for this delightful and flavorful dish from the south of France. At the restaurant, this is used in the recipe for Lamb Diablo.

> *3 medium tomatoes*
> *Salt and white pepper*
> *1 cup Bread Crumbs Provençale (page 188)*

Preheat the oven to 350 degrees.

Remove the stems of the tomatoes and cut the tomatoes in half. Season to taste with salt and white pepper, then cover with the bread crumbs Provençale. Bake in the oven for 12 minutes. Remove and serve immediately.

White Rice
Yields 8 cups

Across Louisiana, there are thousands of occasions calling for white rice—and seemingly as many ways to cook it. This is not only Arnaud's method—it's one that will work for you.

2½ cups long-grain white rice
1 tablespoon salt
1 Bouquet Garni (page 231)
¼ cup (½ stick) butter

Preheat oven to 350 degrees. Rinse the rice in cold water and place it in an ovenproof pot. Add water to a level twice the height of the rice. Add the salt and the bouquet garni and bring to a boil on the stove top over high heat.

Remove from the burner, cover, and cook in the oven for 18 minutes. When the rice is cooked, remove the bouquet garni. Add the butter in small pieces and stir until it is melted and has coated the rice.

Salads

Watercress à la Germaine
Serves 6

Many of Germaine Wells' contributions to Arnaud's menu have fallen by the wayside, either because of questionable inspiration or changing public taste. Yet this simple salad, one of her earliest creations, continues to find an enthusiastic audience.

3 bunches watercress, cleaned
2 cups sliced mushrooms

¾ cup Watercress Dressing (recipe below)
12 cherry tomatoes

Place the watercress on each of 6 salad plates, top with the mushrooms, and add the dressing. Garnish each plate with 2 cherry tomatoes and serve.

Watercress Dressing
Yields 1 cup

½ cup Mayonnaise (page 230)
¼ cup sour cream
⅛ cup Creole cream cheese (see Note below)
¼ tablespoon crushed green peppercorns
⅛ cup chopped green onions or scallions
¼ tablespoon Worcestershire sauce
⅛ teaspoon Tabasco
Salt and white pepper

Using a mixer at low speed, blend the Mayonnaise, sour cream, and cream cheese for 3 minutes, then add the crushed peppercorns along with the green onions or scallions, the Worcestershire sauce, and Tabasco. Blend for 3 minutes. Season to taste with salt and white pepper.

NOTE: Creole cream cheese is the only cheese ever invented in New Orleans—and indeed its precise culture can be duplicated nowhere else. If the real thing (a single large curd surrounded by cream) is unavailable in your area, pour heavy cream over either farmer cheese or large-curd cottage cheese.

Chef's Salad
_____ Serves 6 _____

At Arnaud's, as elsewhere, it is a tradition that the chef devise a special salad. Though this one includes some standard ingredients, it draws distinction from two types of lettuce, apple strips, and the carefully prepared vinaigrette.

> *18 leaves of Boston lettuce*
> *1 1/4 cups chopped romaine lettuce*
> *3 cups julienned Swiss cheese*
> *3 cups julienned ham*
> *2 cups poached and julienned chicken*
> *3 cups julienned apple with peel*
> *3 hard-boiled eggs, sliced crossways*
> *6 tomato wedges*
> *1/4 cup chopped fresh parsley*
> *1 1/2 cups Vinaigrette Dressing (recipe below)*

Arrange 3 Boston lettuce leaves inside each of 6 salad bowls, then place about 6 tablespoons of romaine in the center.

In a separate bowl, mix the cheese, ham, chicken, and apple. Place 1/6 of this mixture on top of each mound of romaine. Decorate with the egg slices, tomato wedges, and chopped parsley. Top with the vinaigrette and serve.

Vinaigrette Dressing
_____ Yields 1 1/2 cups _____

> *1/2 cup red wine vinegar*
> *1/2 tablespoon Dijon mustard*
> *Salt and white pepper*
> *1/2 cup salad oil*

In a bowl, blend the vinegar, mustard, salt, and pepper with a wire whisk. Continue whisking while slowly adding the oil. Whisk until blended, then season to taste with salt and white pepper.

Chicken Salad
Serves 6

Three types of lettuce add interest to the shredded poached chicken, while the red pimentos and green onions join cherry tomatoes for color in what is far from the traditional chicken salad.

18 Boston lettuce leaves
3 cups chopped romaine lettuce
3 cups chopped iceberg lettuce
2 unpeeled apples, thinly sliced
3 cups shredded poached chicken, chilled
3 cups chopped green onions or scallions
3/4 cup chopped red pimentos
7 1/2 hearts of palm, sliced once lengthwise, then cut into
*   1/8-inch slices*
3 hard-boiled eggs, sliced crossways
18 cherry tomatoes
3 cups sliced fresh mushrooms
1 1/2 cups Vinaigrette Dressing (recipe above)

Arrange 3 Boston lettuce leaves inside each of 6 salad bowls. Mix the romaine and iceberg together in a separate bowl and place approximately ½ cup in the center of the Boston lettuce leaves in each of the bowls.

In a separate bowl, mix the apples, chicken, green onions or scallions, pimentos, and hearts of palm. Place ⅙ of this mixture on top of each romaine-iceberg mound. Decorate with the egg slices and cherry tomatoes. Sprinkle with the sliced mushrooms. Top with the vinaigrette and serve.

Crabmeat Salad
—————————————— *Serves 6* ——————————————

This wouldn't be a representative selection of New Orleans salads without at least one celebrating the succulent local lump crabmeat. With plenty of color, and capers for an added taste, this salad handles the assignment in high style.

>*18 Boston lettuce leaves*
>*3 cups chopped romaine lettuce*
>*6 cups fresh lump crabmeat*
>*¾ cup chopped red pimentos*
>*1½ cups sliced mushrooms*
>*1½ cups chopped celery*
>*3 cups chopped green onions or scallions*
>*12 tomato wedges*
>*1 cup small nonpariel capers*
>*¼ cup chopped fresh parsley*
>*1½ cups Vinaigrette Dressing (page 204)*

Arrange 3 Boston lettuce leaves inside each of 6 salad bowls, then place a bit less than ½ cup of chopped romaine in the center.

In a separate bowl, mix the crabmeat, pimentos, mushrooms, celery, and green onions or scallions. Place ⅙ of this mixture atop each mound of romaine. Decorate with the tomato wedges, capers, and chopped parsley. Top with the vinaigrette and serve.

Mixed Green Salad
—————————————— *Serves 6* ——————————————

This simple collection of mixed greens topped with Arnaud's delicate vinaigrette is a model of unabashed cool crispness.

1 head Boston lettuce, shredded
1 head iceberg lettuce, shredded
1 head romaine lettuce, shredded
1 cup peeled and shredded carrots
2 cups shredded red cabbage
2 hard-boiled eggs, chopped
¾ cup Vinaigrette Dressing (page 204)
¼ cup chopped fresh parsley
12 cherry tomatoes

Combine the chilled greens in a large bowl, add the vinaigrette, and toss. Distribute the mixture evenly among 6 salad plates and top with the carrots, cabbage, and eggs. Sprinkle with the chopped parsley, garnish with 2 cherry tomatoes per salad, and serve.

Salade Niçoise
Serves 6

All along the sun-splashed French Riviera, they devour this green salad blessed with the bounty of the South. Luckily, all the same ingredients are available here.

18 Boston lettuce leaves
3 cups chopped romaine lettuce
1½ cups boiled, sliced, and quartered potatoes
3 cups boiled and halved green beans, preferably haricots
  verts
3 cups shredded tuna fish
1 cup pitted California black olives
24 anchovies (whole fillets)
3 hard-boiled eggs, sliced crossways
6 tomato wedges
¼ cup chopped fresh parsley
1½ cups Vinaigrette Dressing (page 204)

Arrange 3 Boston lettuce leaves inside each of 6 salad bowls and place a bit less than ½ cup chopped romaine in the center. On top of the romaine, place alternate layers of the potatoes, beans, and tuna.

Decorate with the olives, anchovies, eggs, and tomato wedges. Sprinkle with the parsley, top with the vinaigrette, and serve.

Pasta Salad
_____ Serves 6 _____

New Orleans' energetic Italian population has contributed to the city's character since the turn of the century. But only the pasta here is Italian. The fresh seafood and zesty mustard dressing are definitely Creole.

18 Boston lettuce leaves
3 cups chopped romaine lettuce
4½ cups cooked elbow macaroni
3 cups medium-size (40–50 count) Boiled Shrimp (page 233)
1⅓ cups fresh lump crabmeat
¾ cup chopped red pimentos
3 cups chopped green onions or scallions
1½ cups Pasta Salad Dressing (recipe below)
Salt and freshly ground black pepper
¼ cup chopped fresh parsley
12 cherry tomatoes

Arrange 3 Boston lettuce leaves inside each of 6 salad bowls. Place just under ½ cup chopped romaine in the center of the Boston leaves.

In another bowl, mix the macaroni, shrimp, crabmeat, red pimentos, and green onions or scallions with the pasta salad dressing. Season to taste with salt and pepper. Place ⅙ of this mixture on top of each romaine mound. Decorate with the chopped parsley and cherry tomatoes, and serve.

Pasta Salad Dressing

Yields 1 1/2 cups

1 1/4 cups Mayonnaise (page 230)
1/4 cup Dijon mustard
1/4 cup white wine vinegar

Using a wire whisk, mix all the ingredients thoroughly before using on pasta salad.

Desserts

Bananas Foster

——— *Serves 6* ———

This is the granddaddy of New Orleans' flaming desserts.. It is surprisingly simple to make, especially over a gas flame. It takes a bit more effort (and a long-stemmed match) to make the magic on an electric range. But it can be done.

> 1¼ *tablespoons ground cinnamon*
> ¾ *tablespoon white granulated sugar*

6 tablespoons (¾ stick) butter
3 cups light brown sugar
6 whole bananas, peeled and quartered
⅓ cup dark rum
¼ cup banana liqueur
6 scoops vanilla ice cream

Mix the cinnamon and white sugar together and keep for later use. Place the butter and brown sugar in a flambé pan and mash together. Place the pan over a flame and caramelize (melt both ingredients). Add the bananas (flat side down) in the center of the pan. Heat for approximately 1 minute.

Remove from heat and add the dark rum. Return to heat, ignite (either by tilting the pan over a gas flame or using a long-stemmed match), and pour the cinnamon-sugar mixture directly into the flame. As the flame dies, remove from heat and add the banana liqueur. Place the pan over a flame again and mix well.

To serve, place one scoop of vanilla ice cream in each of six champagne glasses. Cover with the banana mixture and serve immediately.

NOTE: To avoid serious accidents, *never* add liquor while the flambé pan is *on* the flame.

Flaming Strawberries Arnaud
—————————————— Serves 6 ——————————————

This dessert adds the Arnaud's name to the flambé hall of fame. It is especially delicious when the summer's first strawberries start coming in.

½ cup (1 stick) butter
1 cup sliced almonds
2 tablespoons brandy
¾ cup sugar

2 cups puréed strawberries
2 pints whole strawberries, cleaned
2 tablespoons Grand Marnier
6 scoops vanilla ice cream
1 cup whipped cream

In a sauté pan, melt half the butter over high heat. Sauté the almonds until they are brown. Remove from heat. Pull the almonds to the back of the pan, flame with half the brandy, and mix the almonds up. Put aside.

In a bowl, mix the sugar with the puréed strawberries. Put the mixture in a sauté pan over a flame and add the remaining butter. Mix it up in the purée until it melts down. Make sure the mixture is nice and hot. Add the whole strawberries to the purée and mix. Add the Grand Marnier and mix. Remove from heat. Pull the strawberries to the back of the pan, heat the edge of the pan, and flame with the rest of the brandy.

Serve over the ice cream in individual serving dishes. Add the whipped cream on top and sprinkle the roasted almonds over it.

NOTE: To avoid serious accidents, *never* add liquor while the flambé pan is *on* the flame.

Cherries Jubilee
Serves 6

Thanks in large part to the tart cherries, this dessert is not quite as sweet as those flaming delights made with bananas or strawberries. The sauce should be dark and syrupy-rich.

½ cup granulated sugar
2 cups canned pitted Bing cherries
Zest of 1 orange (optional)
½ Cup Grand Marnier

1/3 cup kirsch
6 scoops vanilla ice cream

Combine the sugar and cherries in a flambé pan, reserving the syrup. Add zest to taste, if desired. Stir the cherries over a high flame to melt the sugar. Remove from flame, add the Grand Marnier, and flame.

Return to flame, and add the reserved cherry syrup. Remove from flame and add the kirsch. Flame, and mix well.

To serve, place one scoop of vanilla ice cream in each of six champagne glasses. Cover with the cherry mixture and serve immediately.

NOTE: To avoid serious accidents, *never* add liquor while the flambé pan is *on* the flame.

Crêpes Suzette
_____ Serves 6 _____

Several Arnaud's waiters have adopted this dessert as their specialty, even though it was created in Monte Carlo in 1898. The crêpes are carefully flamed, then served as a delicate blend of tart and sweet.

1/4 cup (1/2 stick) butter
1 cup granulated sugar
1 orange
1/2 lemon
1/2 cup Grand Marnier
12 crêpes
1/3 cup brandy

Combine the butter and sugar in the flambé pan. Add orange and lemon zest to taste. Caramelize over a flame (allow all ingredients to melt). Remove from the flame and add the Grand Marnier. Flame and add the juice of the orange and lemon half.

Add the crêpes, four at a time, and simmer approximately 1 minute on each side. Fold the crêpes into quarters and baste. Remove from flame and add the brandy. Flame and serve immediately on preheated dinner plates (2 crêpes per serving, covered with sauce).

NOTE: To avoid serious accidents, *never* add liquor while the flambé pan is *on* the flame.

Strawberries Arnaud
Serves 6

Bananas belong to Foster, of course, and crêpes to Suzette, but it's hard to quibble in New Orleans over the rights to luscious strawberries. This simple dessert is all Arnaud's.

3 cups vanilla ice cream
3 cups sliced fresh strawberries
1 1/2 cups Strawberries Arnaud Sauce (recipe below)
Whipped cream

Place 1 scoop of ice cream in each of 6 champagne glasses and cover the scoop with strawberries. Top with the sauce and decorate with whipped cream.

Strawberries Arnaud Sauce
Yields about 2 cups

This sauce is delicious over fruit cocktail, as well as over Strawberries Arnaud.

2 cups red wine
½ orange, sliced
1 lime, sliced
1 clove
1 cinnamon stick
½ cup sugar

Bring the wine to a boil, then add all the other ingredients and stir for 1 minute. Bring to a boil a second time. Turn the heat off and let the mixture cool for 30 minutes. Strain and refrigerate until needed.

NOTE: Strawberries Arnaud Sauce can be kept, covered, in the refrigerator for up to 2 weeks.

Caramel Custard
_____ *Serves 6* _____

For many years, this was the dessert of choice at Arnaud's—especially in the heyday of the Count. It remains an exemplary version of what the Spanish and Portuguese call *flan*.

Caramel:
½ cup sugar
½ tablespoon lemon juice

Custard:
5 whole eggs
8 egg yolks
¾ cup sugar
1 tablespoon vanilla extract
3 cups milk

Preheat the oven to 300 degrees.
To prepare the caramel, combine the sugar and 1 tablespoon

water in a pan over medium heat, stirring until the sugar is melted. Brush the sides of the pan with lemon juice to avoid crystal formation. Remove the liquid from the heat and ladle quickly into each of six 4-ounce custard cups. Allow to cool and dry completely, about 15 minutes.

To make the custard, combine the eggs, egg yolks, sugar, and vanilla in a large bowl and beat with an electric mixer on medium speed. Set aside. In a pan, scald the milk and add to the egg mixture. Continue to mix until the custard is completely cooled.

Pour the mixture into the custard cups, and place them in a baking pan with water halfway up the sides of the cups. Bake for 40 minutes, or until a knife inserted in the center comes out clean. Remove the cups from the water and cool at room temperature, then refrigerate until needed.

When ready to serve, run a small paring knife around the edge of the cups and invert onto dessert plates.

Crème Brûlée
Serves 6

In this rich variation on caramel custard, the name *brûlée* refers to the broiled brown sugar crust on top. One Arnaud's maitre d' called crème brûlée "flan that's died and gone to heaven."

> *6 egg yolks*
> *1/3 cup white sugar*
> *2 1/2 cups heavy cream*
> *1 tablespoon vanilla extract*
> *3 tablespoons dark brown sugar*

Preheat the oven to 250 degrees. In a bowl, beat the egg yolks and white sugar with a mixer at medium speed. Set aside. In a pan, bring the cream to a boil over medium heat. Remove the cream from the heat immediately and add it to the egg-sugar mixture while continuing to beat. Add the vanilla and continue to beat until the mixture is completely cool.

Pour the cool mixture into six 4-ounce custard cups. Line the sides of a 3-inch-high baking pan with parchment paper, then place the cups in the pan. Add water until it reaches halfway up the sides of the cups. (The paper will stabilize the water and prevent the cups from shaking.)

Bake for 50 minutes. Remove the cups from the pan, allow to cool at room temperature, then refrigerate until chilled.

When chilled, evenly spread ½ tablespoon of dark brown sugar over the mixture in each cup. Place the cups on a sheet pan and set under the broiler until the sugar melts, darkens and forms a crust, 20 to 30 seconds. This is the *brulée* process. Refrigerate until ready to serve.

Bread Pudding
Serves 6

Creole housewives, faced with mountains of day-old French bread, came up with what is arguably the best bread pudding in the world. Arnaud's, in turn, perfected the whiskey sauce which crowns it.

> *5 whole eggs*
> *1 egg yolk*
> *½ cup sugar*
> *2 cups milk*
> *1 cup heavy cream*
> *4 tablespoons cinnamon*
> *⅛ teaspoon nutmeg*
> *1 tablespoon vanilla extract*
> *12 ounces day-old French bread*
> *2 tablespoons (¼ stick) butter*
> *2 cups raisins, sprinkled with a small amount of rum*

4 slices white loaf bread
1¹/₂ cups Whiskey Sauce (recipe below)

Preheat the oven to 300 degrees.

Beat the eggs and sugar in a large mixing bowl at medium speed. Add the milk and heavy cream and blend, then cut the mixer speed to low. Add two tablespoons of the cinnamon, along with the nutmeg and vanilla, and blend.

Cut the French bread into small slices. Lightly butter a cake pan 9 inches square and 2 inches deep, then sprinkle the bottom with 2 teaspoons of the remaining cinnamon and ⅔ cup raisins. Spread a layer of bread over the raisins and cover it with one-third of the custard mixture.

Make sure the custard soaks in completely by pressing the bread down with your hands, making sure it absorbs all it can. Repeat the sequence (cinnamon, raisins, bread, custard) twice more, to produce three complete layers in all. Top with the 4 loaf slices and press them down, to make sure the bread is soaked with custard. Sprinkle with additional cinnamon if desired.

Cover the pudding with lightly buttered heavy-duty aluminum foil. Place the cake pan inside a baking dish filled with water halfway up the sides, and bake for 1 hour. Serve warm, topped with 4 tablespoons of warm whiskey sauce per portion.

Whiskey Sauce
Yields about 2 cups

3 eggs
1 cup (2 sticks) butter, melted and still warm
¹/₂ cup granulated sugar
1¹/₂ teaspoons bourbon whiskey

Using a mixer, whip the eggs at high speed until soft peaks form. Reduce the mixer to low speed and slowly add the warm melted butter. Add the sugar slowly and mix until cool, then slowly add the whiskey. Blend thoroughly.

NOTE: Whiskey sauce can be stored, covered, at room temperature for 3 to 4 days.

Chocolate Mousse
Serves 6

Though hardly Creole in its origins, this creamy dessert is well appreciated in the heart of this Creole capital. Arnaud's sets its version apart by dispensing it through a star-shaped pastry tip and sprinkling it with chocolate vermicelli.

> *6¹/₂ ounces semisweet chocolate (preferably Callebaut)*
> *2 cups plus 1 tablespoon heavy cream*
> *3 tablespoons unsweetened cocoa*
> *2 egg yolks*
> *3 tablespoons granulated sugar*
> *4 egg whites*
> *Chocolate vermicelli for garnish*

Place the chocolate and 1 tablespoon of the cream in the top of a double boiler over low heat. Melt slowly without stirring. In a separate bowl, combine the remaining 2 cups cream and the cocoa and refrigerate until needed.

When the chocolate is melted, remove it from the heat and allow it to cool to room temperature. Place the egg yolks in a large mixing bowl. Over a water bath (a large pan of simmering water), whip the egg yolks and 1 tablespoon of the sugar until the mixture starts to develop streaks and turns pale yellow. Remove from the heat and allow to cool slightly.

In a steady stream, add the chocolate to the egg mixture and blend gently. In another bowl, beat the egg whites with a mixer at medium speed until soft peaks form. Add the remaining 2 tablespoons sugar all at once and whip at high speed until the mixture stiffens.

Fold the egg-white mixture gently into the chocolate-egg mixture, using a rubber spatula. Remove the whipping cream and cocoa from the refrigerator and whip until firm. Fold this gently into the mousse with a rubber spatula until the entire mixture is blended. Refrigerate until needed.

To serve, dispense the mousse into six 4-ounce custard cups using a pastry bag with a star-shaped tip. Garnish with chocolate vermicelli and serve.

Cheesecake

Serves 10 to 12

At the start of the Casbarian era, Arnaud's purchased its pastries from independent bakers. As the restaurant assumed control over more and more of its production, this American classic emerged as a winner.

> *1 cup graham cracker crumbs*
> *¹/₂ cup (1 stick) butter, softened at room temperature*
> *¹/₄ cup blanched sliced almonds*
> *¹/₂ cup plus 2 tablespoons granulated sugar*
> *2 8-ounce packages of cream cheese, softened at room*
>   *temperature*
> *1¹/₂ cups sour cream*
> *4 whole eggs*
> *4 egg yolks*
> *1 tablespoon vanilla extract*

1 tablespoon lemon juice
¾ cup Strawberry Sauce (recipe below)

Preheat the oven to 275 degrees.

In a 9-by-2-inch round cake pan, combine the graham cracker crumbs, softened butter, almonds, and two tablespoons of the sugar. Blend well by hand and flatten the mixture thinly on the bottom and sides of the pan. Refrigerate for later use.

Using a mixer, combine the softened cream cheese and sour cream in a large mixing bowl. Whip on medium speed until the mixture is well-blended and free of lumps. Add the remaining ½ cup sugar, and the eggs, egg yolks, vanilla, and lemon juice, and continue to mix on low speed for 10 minutes.

Allow the mixture to rest about 10 minutes to eliminate any bubbles from the mixing, then pour into the chilled graham cracker crust.

Bake in the oven for 1 hour, or until an inserted paring knife comes out clean. Refrigerate at least 8 hours or overnight before serving.

When ready to serve, cut the cheesecake into 6 portions, place each on a dessert plate, and top with approximately 2 tablespoons of the strawberry sauce.

Strawberry Sauce
Yields ¾ cup

1 cup fresh strawberries
½ cup granulated sugar
1 tablespoon vanilla extract
1 tablespoon kirsch

Combine all the ingredients in a saucepan and stir over medium heat for 10 minutes. Blend into a purée, then allow to cool before using.

Creole Cream Cheese Evangeline
_____ Serves 6 _____

This cooling fruit salad is named for both Creoles and Cajuns (Evangeline was one of the latter, of course). It is accented by a delightful sauce of Creole cream cheese, cream, sugar, and vanilla.

> 2 apples, peeled, cored, and diced
> 2 pears, peeled, cored, and diced
> 2 oranges, peeled, sectioned, and white pith removed
> 2 bananas, peeled and sliced
> 1 cup strawberries, washed and halved
> 1 1/2 cups seedless grapes, red or white
> 5 tablespoons granulated sugar
> 3 tablespoons Cointreau
> 2 packages Creole cream cheese, 11 ounces each (see Note on
>   page 203)
> 1 cup heavy cream
> 1/2 teaspoon vanilla extract
> 6 fresh mint leaves

Combine all the fruit in a large bowl, then mix in 2 tablespoons of the sugar and the Cointreau. Refrigerate for 1 hour.

In a separate bowl, using a mixer, blend the cream cheese, cream, vanilla, and the remaining 3 tablespoons sugar.

When ready to serve, place the fruit salad in 6 glass cups and cover with the sauce. Decorate with mint leaves.

Fresh Fruit Cocktail
_____ Serves 6 _____

At the height of a New Orleans summer, "cold" is just about the best thing you can say about any food or beverage. This simple presentation doubles as a light but colorful dessert and a popular appetizer at Arnaud's jazz brunch.

> 2 bananas, peeled and sliced
> 1 1/2 pears, peeled, cored, and diced
> 1 orange, peeled, sectioned, and white pith removed
> 1 1/2 apples, peeled, cored, and diced
> 1 1/2 cups strawberries, washed and halved
> 4 1/4 cups seedless grapes, red or white
> 1/2 cup granulated sugar
> 2 tablespoons Cointreau liqueur

Combine all the fruit in a bowl. Add the sugar and Cointreau and mix well. Refrigerate for 15 to 20 minutes. Serve in 6 champagne glasses.

Basic Recipes

Béarnaise Sauce

Yields 1 1/2 cups

This traditional French sauce is a miracle for meats. At Arnaud's, it is used with Charlemond Sauce on the Filet Mignon of that name and with Bordelaise on Chicken Rochambeau. The preparation of clarified butter is noted below.

1/2 cup red wine vinegar
1/2 cup chopped fresh tarragon

¹/₄ cup chopped shallots
¹/₂ teaspoon coarsely ground black pepper
5 egg yolks
1¹/₄ cups (2¹/₂ sticks) butter, clarified
Salt and white pepper

In a medium saucepan, combine the vinegar, tarragon, shallots, and pepper. Boil over high heat until the liquid evaporates, leaving a moist mixture. Remove from the heat. Allow to cool until barely warm.

Transfer the mixture to the top of a double boiler. Add the egg yolks and whisk until a pale yellow ribbon starts to form. Add the clarified butter very slowly while continuing to whisk. Season to taste with salt and white pepper.

NOTE: To make clarified butter, melt the butter over low heat to keep it from browning. Using a spoon, skim off all the white froth that rises to the top, then carefully pour the yellow "clarified" portion from the pan into a container. Clarified butter may be kept refrigerated for 2 to 3 weeks.

Béchamel Sauce
———————————— Yields 1 quart ————————————

Here's a classic French preparation that at Arnaud's provides the soul for three of the most popular soups—Cream of Artichoke, Cream of Asparagus, and Cream of Broccoli. Of course, it's also wonderful on its own.

1 quart milk
1 cup sliced white onions
1 Bouquet Garni (page 231)
1 clove
1 bay leaf
Salt and white pepper
1 cup Roux (page 232)

Place the milk, onions, bouquet garni, clove, and bay leaf in a saucepan and bring to a boil. Season to taste with salt and white pepper, then, using a wire whisk, gradually thicken with the roux, a little at a time, until the sauce coats a spoon. Strain.

NOTE: Béchamel sauce can be kept, covered, in the refrigerator for 3 to 4 days.

Bordelaise Sauce
Yields about 2 cups

For sheer versatility, it's hard to beat this sauce. It turns up at Arnaud's over, under, or around Eggs Hussarde, Chicken Rochambeau, Twelfth Night Cornish Game Hen, Stuffed Quail au Chambertin, Sweetbreads Eleanor, Grillades and Grits, and Tips of Filet en Brochette.

2 tablespoons (1/4 stick) butter
1/4 cup chopped shallots
1 cup red wine
1 Bouquet Garni (page 231)
1 clove
1 black peppercorn
1/2 clove garlic, skin on
1 quart Veal Stock (page 237)
1 tablespoon Roux (page 232)
Salt and freshly ground black pepper

Melt the butter in a pan over high heat, then add the shallots and cook until translucent. Add the red wine and bring to a boil, then add the bouquet garni, cloves, peppercorns, garlic, and veal stock. Reduce the heat and simmer until the volume is reduced by half.

Thicken by gradually adding the roux until the sauce coats a spoon. Strain, then season to taste with salt and pepper.

NOTE: Bordelaise sauce can be kept, covered, in the refrigerator for up to 1 week.

Creole Sauce
_____ Yields 1 quart _____

Sharing its name with a world-famous cuisine, this sauce had better be special. And it is just that when served with Shrimp Creole, Chicken Creole, or Grillades and Grits.

> 1/8 cup olive oil
> 1 cup chopped white onions
> 1/2 cup diced green peppers
> 1 1/2 cups chopped celery
> 1/2 cup chopped fresh parsley
> 1 clove garlic, chopped
> 1/2 quart Veal Stock (page 237)
> 1/4 tablespoon chicken base, or dehydrated bouillon
> 1 Bouquet Garni (page 231)
> 1/2 cup diced tomatoes
> 1 1/2 cups tomato purée
> Salt and freshly ground black pepper
> Tabasco
> Cayenne

Heat the olive oil in a pot over high heat, then add the onions, green peppers, celery, and parsley. Stir for 2 minutes, then add the garlic. Add the veal stock, chicken base or bouillon, bouquet garni, diced tomatoes, and tomato purée and bring to a boil.

Reduce the heat and simmer for 10 minutes. Season to taste with salt, black pepper, Tabasco, and cayenne.

NOTE: Creole sauce can be kept, covered, in the refrigerator for 2 to 3 days, or frozen.

Hollandaise Sauce
———————————— Yields about 2 cups ————————————

While among the best-known French sauces, hollandaise is one of the least agreed-upon in terms of technique. Here is Arnaud's method, showcased so elegantly over egg dishes at brunch.

6 egg yolks
2 cups (4 sticks) butter, melted
Salt and white pepper
Cayenne pepper
1 tablespoon lemon juice

Combine the egg yolks and 1½ tablespoons water in the top of a double boiler and whip with a wire whisk over hot (but not boiling) water until fluffy. Slowly add the butter, whipping continuously until it blends and the sauce begins to thicken.

Add salt, white pepper, and cayenne to taste, then whisk in the lemon juice.

Armoricaine Sauce
———————————— Yields 1 quart ————————————

This sauce, a bit unusual but a French classic nonetheless, is a favorite of Arnaud's chefs. Its rich flavors come from the south of France—shellfish, olive oil, tomatoes, and garlic—all direct links to the Creoles. It is delicious over fish, shellfish, or veal.

2 pounds crawfish, with shell still on (live if possible)
⅛ cup olive oil
⅜ cup chopped shallots
⅛ cup chopped white onions
⅛ cup sliced carrots

⅛ *cup chopped celery*
⅛ *cup chopped leeks*
⅛ *cup brandy*
3 *tablespoons white wine*
1 *tablespoon tomato purée*
1 *tomato, whole*
1½ *cloves garlic, whole*
2 *cloves*
⅛ *teaspoon black peppercorns*
1 *cup Fish Stock (page 239)*
1 *teaspoon prepared lobster base (optional, available in gourmet shops)*
1 *quart water*
2 *tablespoons Roux (page 232)*
Salt and freshly ground black pepper
Cayenne pepper

Wash the crawfish several times to make sure they are thoroughly clean. In a large pot, heat the olive oil to the smoking point over high heat, then add the crawfish and cook until they become deep red. Add the shallots, onions, carrots, celery, and leeks and stir 3 to 4 minutes.

Add the brandy and flame for 10 seconds, extinguishing it by placing the cover over the pot. Add the white wine, tomato purée, whole tomato, garlic, cloves, and peppercorns. Stir, then add the fish stock, lobster base, if using, and water. Bring to a boil, reduce the heat, cover, and simmer for 30 minutes.

Transfer the mixture to a blender and mix for 2 minutes. Return it to the pot and boil for 7 to 10 minutes more, then thicken by adding the roux, 1 tablespoon at a time, until the sauce coats a spoon. Strain through a strainer and season to taste with salt, pepper, and cayenne.

NOTE: Armoricaine sauce can be kept, covered, in the refrigerator for up to 4 days.

Cocktail Sauce
_____ *Yields about 2 cups* _____

It's hard not to love a good cocktail sauce when the seafood is cold and fresh. This version is used at Arnaud's with the Crabmeat Cocktail and with Oysters on the Half Shell.

> *1 cup salsa-style chili sauce*
> *¾ cup ketchup*
> *¼ cup horseradish*
> *¼ cup chopped white onions*
> *¼ teaspoon chopped garlic*
> *1 tablespoon lemon juice*
> *¼ cup canned or bottled tomato juice*
> *2–3 drops Tabasco*
> *1 tablespoon brandy*
> *Salt and white pepper*

Using a mixer at low speed, blend the chili sauce, ketchup, and horseradish for 3 minutes. Add the onions and garlic and blend for 1 minute. Pour in the lemon juice, tomato juice, and Tabasco and blend for 1 minute. Add the brandy along with salt and white pepper to taste, blending the cocktail sauce 1 minute more.

NOTE: Cocktail sauce can be kept, covered, in the refrigerator for up to 1 week.

Mayonnaise
_____ *Yields about 2 cups* _____

Though most Americans grow up with a jar of store-bought mayonnaise in the refrigerator, more and more are making their own these days.

The reason is taste, pure and simple. And the difference it makes when used in cooking reduces the effort to minimal.

> *3 egg yolks*
> *2 tablespoons Dijon mustard*
> *1 pinch of salt*
> *1 pinch of white pepper*
> *2 cups vegetable oil*

Using your mixer at low speed, combine the egg yolks, mustard, salt, and pepper and beat until the mixture is fluffy. Add the oil slowly in a thin stream while continuing to beat until all the oil is used and the mayonnaise is thick.

NOTE: This mayonnaise can be kept, covered, in the refrigerator for up to 1 week.

Bouquet Garni

Here is the classic method for preparing seasonings so they can be easily retrieved from a completed stock or sauce.

> *½ bunch parsley*
> *3 bay leaves*
> *1 branch fresh thyme*
> *1 stalk celery*

Tie the ingredients together with butcher's twine and use as needed.

Roux

Yields 2 cups

There are as many types of roux in south Louisiana as there are restaurants and home kitchens. Here is Arnaud's version of the traditional Creole thickening agent.

> *1 cup (2 sticks) butter*
> *2 cups flour*

Melt the butter in a small pot over high heat, then add the flour gradually, stirring constantly with a wire whisk. Cook until the mixture becomes a paste. Remove from the heat and store covered at room temperature until needed.

NOTE: Do not refrigerate roux. It can be successfully kept for up to about a week. This recipe can be halved.

Sautéed Crabmeat

Yields 4 cups

There was a time when this was a menu selection for diners with the simplest of tastes. Today it is only an essential part of several more elaborate preparations. Sautéeing crabmeat properly, and not overcooking it, is an important skill at Arnaud's.

> *1½ cups Garlic Butter (page 241)*
> *1½ cups finely chopped green onions*
> *2 pounds fresh lump crabmeat*
> *Salt and white pepper*

Melt the butter in a pan over low heat, then add the green onions and the crabmeat. Stir gently, only until the mixture is heated through. Be careful not to overcook. Season to taste with salt and pepper.

Boiled Crawfish Tails
Yields 1 cup

When Louisianians want to devour boiled crawfish, they cook them up with plenty of hot pepper and other spices. So this formula for boiling the shellfish is intended only for recipes in which they are sauced, such as Crawfish O'Connor and Crawfish Wellington at Arnaud's.

3 pounds live crawfish
4 quarts Courtbouillon (page 234)

Purge the crawfish in a tub of cold water, then repeat the process twice, changing the water each time.

Place the courtbouillon in a large pot and bring to a boil over high heat. Add the crawfish and cook for 7 minutes, then remove from the heat and drain. Allow to cool, then peel them and reserve the tails.

NOTE: Prior to boiling, mud and other debris should be removed from the crawfish by washing them with cool fresh water. There is a tradition around Louisiana that a box of table salt added to the water helps this "purging" along, but commercial processors have determined that a simple water bath is good enough.

Boiled Shrimp
Yields 2¹/₂ pounds

Most of the boiled shrimp in New Orleans are served spicy on tables covered with newspaper. But in a fine Creole dish, these spices can clash with the sauce. So here is a boiling method for shrimp destined to play a part in Arnaud's dishes. It takes about 3½ pounds of whole fresh shrimp to yield 2½ pounds headless, peeled, and deveined.

> *1 stick celery, leaves on, cut into 3 pieces*
> *½ white onion, cut into 2 pieces*
> *3 cloves*
> *1 carrot, coarsely sliced*
> *3 bay leaves*
> *3½ pounds uncooked fresh shrimp (40–50 count), or 2½*
> *pounds frozen, headless, peeled shrimp*

Combine 12 quarts water and all the ingredients except the shrimp in a large pot and bring to a boil over high heat. Add the shrimp and return the contents to a boil. Continue cooking for 2 to 3 minutes, until the shrimp turn pink. Remove from the heat, drain the shrimp, and allow them to cool. If using fresh shrimp, remove heads, peel, and devein.

Poached Eggs
Yields 12

Since all the sauce in the world can't save a badly poached egg, here is the way Arnaud's handles the task for its flourish of elegant brunch dishes. You may poach the eggs in advance and reheat them in salted boiling water for about 30 seconds before serving.

> *3 tablespoons white vinegar*
> *1 teaspoon salt*
> *12 eggs, at room temperature*

Combine water to cover, the vinegar, and the salt in a skillet and bring to a boil over high heat, then reduce the heat to a simmer immediately. Break the eggs one at a time into a saucer and slip them gently into the water. Let the eggs steep until the whites are firm, about 2 minutes, then remove them with a slotted spoon. Drain briefly on absorbent paper and trim with a sharp knife.

Courtbouillon
_____ *Yields 4 quarts* _____

Here is the secret to a flavorful poaching liquid, the kind that works wonders with the fish in several Arnaud's dishes and with the main ingredient in Sweetbreads Eleanor. It can also be used for poaching chicken.

1 carrot, sliced
3 stalks celery, sliced
½ small white onion, sliced
3 bay leaves
3 cloves
½ teaspoon whole black peppercorns
⅛ cup salt

Combine the ingredients in a pot with 4 quarts water and bring to a boil over high heat. Boil for about 6 minutes so the vegetables and seasonings can flavor the water. Add the item to be poached and cook as specified in the individual recipe.

NOTE: Courtbouillon can be kept successfully in the refrigerator for up to a week.

Chicken Stock

_____ Yields 4 quarts _____

Chicken stock has to be one of the most useful things to keep around the home kitchen. Many recipes that call for canned broth can be noticeably improved with the substitution of your own homemade stock.

> 2 pounds chicken bones
> 1 cup chopped carrots
> 1/2 cup chopped onions
> 1/2 cup chopped celery
> 1 Bouquet Garni (page 231)
> 2 teaspoons juniper berries
> Pinch of whole thyme
> Salt and white pepper

Preheat the oven to 400 degrees.

Place the bones in a roasting pan and brown them in the oven for 15 to 20 minutes.

In a large stockpot, bring 8 quarts water to a boil over high heat. Add the bones, vegetables, bouquet garni, juniper berries, thyme, and salt and white pepper to taste. Return to a boil, then reduce the heat and simmer for 1 hour, until the liquid is reduced by half. Strain the stock and allow it to cool completely. Refrigerate, covered, until needed.

NOTE: Chicken stock can be kept in the refrigerator for 3 to 4 days.

Duck Stock

_____ Yields 4 quarts _____

To make this stock, it's best to be a duck hunter or be friends with one. If you are neither, the bones can be acquired from the whole ducks you buy or from the people who cut up and debone them.

2 pounds duck bones
1 cup chopped carrots
½ cup chopped onions
½ cup chopped celery
1 Bouquet Garni (page 231)
2 teaspoons juniper berries
Pinch of whole thyme
Salt and white pepper

Preheat the oven to 400 degress.

Place the bones in a roasting pan and brown in the oven for 15 to 20 minutes.

Place 8 quarts water in a stockpot and bring to a boil over high heat. Add the bones, vegetables, bouquet garni, juniper berries, thyme, and salt and white pepper to taste. Bring to a boil, reduce the heat, and simmer for 1 hour, until the stock is reduced by half. Strain and allow to cool completely. Refrigerate, covered, until needed.

NOTE: Duck stock can be kept in the refrigerator for 3 to 4 days.

Veal Stock
———————————— *Yields 1 quart* ————————————

This might just be the most important stock at Arnaud's. It is used to make the sauce for the Count's famous Trout Meunière, as well as sauces for several popular veal dishes.

2 pounds veal bones
1 ounce rock salt
2⅔ cups sliced onions
2 cups sliced carrots
1 cup sliced leeks
1⅓ cups sliced celery

1 cup chopped fresh parsley
1 teaspoon dried thyme
2 bay leaves
½ head garlic, peeled
½ cup tomato purée
5 black peppercorns

Preheat the oven to 450 degrees.

Place the veal bones in a roasting pan, sprinkle with the rock salt, and bake until brown in order to extract the most flavor, about ½ hour. Then place the bones, 8 quarts water, and all the other ingredients in a stockpot and bring to a boil over high heat.

Reduce the heat and simmer for 2 to 3 hours, skimming as needed. When the stock is done, strain it through a strainer, return it to the pot, and reduce it over high heat to one-third its volume.

The stock can be kept in the refrigerator for up to a week.

Shrimp Stock

——————————— *Yields 2 quarts* ———————————

This is one of the easiest stocks to make, and it rises to great heights in Arnaud's recipe for Gumbo.

2 quarts Courtbouillon (page 234)
1¼ pounds raw shrimp, in their shells

Place the courtbouillon in a large pot and bring to a boil over high heat. Add the shrimp and cook for 3 minutes. Remove from the heat and strain. Save the shrimp for another dish.

NOTE: Shrimp stock can be kept in the refrigerator for 3 to 4 days.

Fish Stock

Yields 3 quarts

Some home cooks prefer to buy stocks commercially in whatever form or whatever quality they can find. But Arnaud's believes a rich stock is the heart and soul of a sauce, and the sauces in turn make the dishes. This one is surprisingly quick and easy labor.

1 pound fish bones
1/2 cup chopped shallots
1/2 leek, chopped
1/2 cup chopped celery
1/2 cup chopped fresh parsley
1 pinch dried thyme
1 bay leaf
3 black peppercorns
1/2 cup white wine
3 quarts water

Wash the fish bones several times to make sure they are thoroughly clean. Place the bones with the vegetables and seasonings in a 2-gallon pot, then add the wine and the water and bring to a boil.

Reduce the heat and simmer for 15 minutes. Remove from the heat, skim, and allow to cool. Strain through a strainer.

NOTE: Fish stock can be kept in the refrigerator for 3 to 4 days.

Fish Velouté

Yields 1 quart

In classic French cuisine, velouté is made with either fish stock or chicken stock and is used as the basis for most white wine sauces. At Arnaud's, the addition of nutmeg to the salt and white pepper reveals the Creole influence.

¾ cup flour
¼ cup (½ stick) butter
3 cups hot Fish Stock (recipe above)
½ cup heavy cream
Salt and white pepper
Nutmeg

In a pan over high heat, make a roux with the flour and butter and stir until it is light brown. Add the hot fish stock and boil until the reduced liquid coats a spoon. Add the cream and boil for 5 minutes, then season to taste with salt, white pepper, and nutmeg. Strain through a strainer.

NOTE: Fish velouté can be successfully kept in the refrigerator for about 3 days.

Glassage
Yields 2 cups

Glassage is a traditional French glazing technique. At Arnaud's, it is used to great effect on oyster dishes, imparting flavor and giving an enticing fresh shine to their appearance.

¾ cup Fish Velouté (page 239)
1 cup Hollandaise Sauce (page 228)
¼ cup heavy cream

Using your mixer at low speed, add the velouté to the hollandaise. In a separate container, whip the cream until it thickens but does not yet make peaks. Then stir it into the velouté-hollandaise mixture:

Lemon Butter
_____ Yields 1 cup _____

This Arnaud's sauce is quick and easy to make, and it works wonders for a simple grilled chicken breast or a carefully sautéed fillet of fish.

> _¾ cup (1½ sticks) butter_
> _Juice of 1 lemon_
> _Salt and white pepper_
> _2 teaspoons chopped fresh parsley_

Melt the butter in a pan over high heat, then add the lemon juice. Season to taste with salt and white pepper, then add the chopped parsley. Remove from the heat and keep warm until needed.

Garlic Butter
_____ Yields 1½ cups _____

Garlic butter is used at Arnaud's as a reminder of the Provence region of France. Among the dishes to which it contributes are Crab Claws Provençale, Frog Legs Provençale, Shrimp Clemenceau, and Crabmeat Monaco.

> _1⅝ cups (3¼ sticks) butter, softened_
> _1 cup chopped fresh parsley_
> _¼ cup Herbsaint liqueur_
> _⅛ cup chopped garlic_
> _Salt and freshly ground black pepper_

Place the butter in a mixing bowl. Add the parsley, Herbsaint, and garlic, and mix at low speed with a hand-held mixer for 15 minutes. Season to taste with salt and pepper.

NOTE: Covered with plastic wrap, garlic butter can be kept in the refrigerator for up to a week.

Boiled Artichokes
_____ *Serves 6* _____

Several of Arnaud's recipes use boiled artichokes, either the hearts or the bottoms. If you prefer to purchase your artichokes fresh, rather than precooked in a jar or can, here is the method for boiling them. The desired sections can be removed after this process.

2 cups rock salt
6 medium artichokes

Bring 8 quarts water and the rock salt to a boil over high heat. Add the whole artichokes and put a plate into the water to keep them from floating to the top. Cook for 12 to 16 minutes (depending on their size), until the leaves peel away easily. Drain. The leaves will peel off. The heart will pull out and the inside stringy choke can be cleaned out with a teaspoon.

Drinks

New Orleans brings a spectacular flair to its drinking, just as it does to its dining. And well the city should, since the whole notion of cocktails goes back nearly two centuries to these same French Quarter streets. It seems an apothecary named Antoine Amadée Peychaud, who had fled to New Orleans after a bloody uprising on Santo Domingo, took to dispensing a brandy-based cure-all from his establishment on Royal Street. Peychaud eased a new word into the language by serving this welcome relief in the larger side of a double-ended eggcup, known in French as a *coquetier*. With his adopted city's flair for mispronunciation, it became *cock-tay* almost immediately, and finally, cocktail.

French 75

This was one of Count Arnaud's favorites. He often enjoyed it with guests in his restaurant—when he wasn't sipping his beloved 50–50 mix of bourbon and black coffee.

>*1½ ounces gin or vodka, according to your preference*
>*1½ ounces sweet 'n' sour mix*
>*Champagne*
>*1 cherry*

In a shaker, combine the first two ingredients with ice. Shake well. Strain into a chilled champagne glass. Top with champagne and the cherry.

French 95

The Count, Frenchman that he was, loved this blend of two of that country's most famed beverages—cognac and champagne.

>*1½ ounces cognac*
>*1½ ounces sweet 'n' sour mix*
>*Champagne*
>*1 cherry*

In a shaker, combine the first two ingredients with ice. Shake well. Strain into a chilled champagne glass. Top with champagne and the cherry.

Ojen Frappe

Ojen is a Spanish anise liqueur whose flavor is much more subtle than the French. It turns a delightful pink when it mixes with the ice.

> *2 ounces Ojen*
> *1 tablespoon simple syrup (see Note below)*
> *1 ounce club soda*

Combine the ingredients in a highball glass and then add plenty of crushed ice.

NOTE: To make simple syrup (if you cannot find it commercially) combine 1 cup of water with 2 cups of sugar in a pan, bring to a boil, and simmer for 5 minutes. Let cool. Leftover simple syrup can be stored in a closed jar in the refrigerator.

Gin Fizz

One of New Orleans' most legendary drinks, this was invented by a barman named Henry Ramos in the 1880s. When Huey Long was Louisiana's governor, he often traveled to New York with a bartender from New Orleans so he wouldn't have to be without this drink.

> *1½ ounces gin*
> *2 drops orange-flower water, available commercially*
> *1 egg white*
> *1 tablespoon simple syrup (see Note above)*
> *½ teaspoon lemon juice*
> *2 ounces half-and-half*
> *2 ounces milk*

In a shaker, combine all the ingredients with ice. Shake well for 30 seconds. Pour into a chilled champagne glass over ice cubes.

Sazerac

Though Bloody Marys will always have admirers, the Sazerac is New Orleans' favorite eye-opener. Invented at the old Sazerac Bar in the French Quarter, the drink is ritualized today by bartenders on morning shifts in every corner of the city.

> *2 ounces rye whiskey*
> *1 teaspoon simple syrup (see Note on page 245)*
> *3 dashes Peychaud bitters*
> *3 dashes Angostura bitters*
> *Splash of water*
> *2 dashes of Herbsaint liqueur*
> *Lemon twist*

Combine all the ingredients, except the Herbsaint and lemon twist, with ice. Stir well. Pour the Herbsaint into a chilled rock glass and coat the interior of the glass. Pour off any excess. Strain the rye mixture into the glass and add a lemon twist.

Absinthe Suissesse

The Old Absinthe House on Bourbon Street—from which Count Arnaud made the money to start his restaurant—long specialized in this frothy drink with the delicate licorice taste. Absinthe is outlawed in the United States today, so substitute Herbsaint.

>*1½ ounces Herbsaint liqueur*
>*1 egg white*
>*3 drops orange-flower water*
>*3 drops white crème de menthe*
>*1 tablespoon simple syrup (see Note on page 245)*
>*2 ounces half-and-half*
>*2 ounces milk*

In a shaker, combine all the ingredients with ice. Shake well. Strain into a chilled stem glass with a little crushed ice.

Brandy Milk Punch

This is the French Quarter's favorite "morning after" drink, since it exhibits such a skill for smoothing over excesses from the night before. The shaking gives it an oh-so-welcome frothiness, while the nutmeg adds a dash of color.

>*1½ ounces brandy*
>*1 tablespoon simple syrup*
>*6 drops vanilla extract*
>*2 ounces half-and-half*
>*2 ounces milk*
>*Nutmeg*

In a shaker, combine all the ingredients except the nutmeg with ice. Shake well. Strain into a chilled highball glass with a lititle ice. Dust with nutmeg.

Café Brûlot
_____ Serves 6 _____

Legend has it that this spectacular Arnaud's coffee beverage was "invented" by New Orleans' beloved buccaneer Jean Lafitte, who discovered all the ingredients aboard his ships. This may not be history, but it should be. In any case, a festive dinner à la Arnaud's demands a finale such as this.

> *¹/₈ cup whole cloves*
> *14 cinnamon sticks, broken*
> *¹/₈ cup granulated sugar*
> *Rind of 1 lemon*
> *1 orange*
> *¹/₂ cup plus 1 tablespoon Grand Marnier*
> *¹/₃ cup plus 1 tablespoon French brandy*
> *4 cups coffee (more, if less sweet Café Brûlot is desired)*

Place the cloves in a brûlot bowl (or stainless steel or silver bowl). Add the cinnamon sticks, sugar, and lemon rind. Using a paring knife, peel the orange in one continual strip, and leave the peel attached to the orange at one end. Stud the orange with the cloves, recoil the peel around it, and place it in the brûlot bowl. Add ½ cup Grand Marnier and ⅓ cup brandy.

Set the brûlot bowl over a flame and allow all the ingredients to heat. Then press a fork into the pulp of the orange, lift it from the bowl, and set it aside momentarily. Pour 1 tablespoon each of Grand Marnier and French brandy into a stainless steel or silver ladle and ignite carefully with a long-stemmed match. With your free hand, pick up the orange on the fork and twirl so the peel twists down into the liquid in the bowl.

Pour the flaming alcohol from the ladle down the peel (lights in the room should be dimmed for this), then twice scoop the ladle down into the bowl for more of the now-flaming mixture and pour it down around the peel. When all the fire burns out, pour the coffee into the bowl. Discard the orange. Serve in New Orleans brûlot mugs or in any decorative coffee cups.

Index

About the Author

John DeMers has been enjoying meals at Arnaud's in New Orleans for as long as he can remember. A native of the city, he is based there as the food editor for United Press International. He has been a food journalist, traveling around the world, sampling and writing about different cuisines for more than fifteen years. He lives outside New Orleans with his wife and two children.